THE
OLD TESTAMENT

NOTES

including
- *Introduction*
- *Outline of Old Testament History*
- *Order of the Writings*
- *Summaries and Commentaries*
- *Chronology*
- *Selected Bibliography*

by
Charles H. Patterson
Professor of Philosophy
University of Nebraska

INCORPORATED
LINCOLN, NEBRASKA 68501

Editor

Gary Carey, M.A.
University of Colorado

Consulting Editor

James L. Roberts, Ph.D.
Department of English
University of Nebraska

Cliffs Notes, Inc.   Lincoln, Nebraska

CONTENTS

Foreword 5

Introduction 5

A Short Outline of Old Testament History 7

A Chronological Order of Writings 16

Summaries and Commentaries
  The Prophetic Books
    Amos 22
    Hosea 26
    Isaiah 30
    Micah 35
    Zepheniah, Nahum, and Habakkuk 37
    Jeremiah 40
    Ezekiel 44
    Deutero-Isaiah 49
    Post-Exilic Prophets 52

  The Historical Writings
    The Pentateuch 56
    Joshua, Judges, and Samuel 63
    Kings, Chronicles, Ezra, and Nehemiah 67

  The Wisdom Literature
    The Book of Job 72
    Ecclesiastes 75
    Proverbs 76

  Miscellaneous Writings
    Jonah, Ruth, and Esther 79
    Daniel 84
    Psalms 87
    Lamentations and the Song of Songs 90

  The Apocrypha and the Pseudepigrapha 92

Important Old Testament Dates 96

Selected Bibliography 96

FOREWORD

This brief collection of notes concerning the Old Testament is designed as a guide to an intelligent reading of one of the great books of the world. It is not intended to be a substitute for reading any of the books of the Bible, nor does it take the place of any of the scholarly works that have been written concerning the origin and meaning of the various books included in the Bible. Its purpose is rather to aid the student who is beginning the study of this important literature and who feels somewhat at a loss to know how to go about it. This feeling is a very common one and the reasons for it are fairly obvious. The Old Testament is not an easy book to read. It is even more difficult to understand. Its contents are not only ancient in origin but they were produced by many different persons who lived and worked under conditions that are foreign to our modern and contemporary society. It is impossible to read the Bible intelligently without some familiarity with the persons who wrote it. One needs to know as much about them as he can, including the conditions under which they lived and the purpose which they hoped to realize in the literature they produced.

The study of the Old Testament is a fascinating subject. It is something that has never been completed by any individual or for that matter by any generation of persons. It is a task which has been going on for centuries and it is one that still challenges the minds of great scholars as well as average laymen. More people are becoming interested in it today than ever before and more people are coming to realize that in spite of its complexities and difficulties the results are very much worthwhile. It is hoped that these notes and summaries will not only aid the student in reading the Old Testament but will stimulate his interest in a further pursuit of the great themes that are presented in it.

INTRODUCTION

Although the Old Testament is often referred to as a book, it is really a collection of many books or separate manuscripts produced by different individuals over a long period of time. They were not all written for the same purpose nor were they considered to be of equal importance at the times when they were written. Many of these writings were in existence in some form long before they were assembled into a single collection and given the status of scripture, or sacred writings. It was not until the sixth and fifth centuries B.C. that any portion of the Old Testament writings were arranged in the form in which we have them today. It was during this period that they came to be regarded as authoritative documents for declaring the word of the deity to the people of Israel. At later times other writings were added to the original collection, but it was not until near the close of the first century A.D. that general agreement was reached concerning all of the books which are now included in the canon of the Old Testament.

The importance of this book as reflected in the influence it has had through the centuries can scarcely be overestimated. Its religious significance is indicated primarily by the fact that it is recognized as a part of the inspired sacred literature of three of the major religions of the world. It was first of all the sacred Bible of Judaism and it is so regarded at the present time. Along with the New Testament, it is included in the Bible of Christianity, and it holds a similar place in the religion of Islam, for the followers of Mohammed accept its teachings along with those of the Koran. The influence of the Old Testament has not been confined to the adherents of these three religions but it has permeated the entire culture of many of the larger countries of the world. It has been one of the main sources of the moral and political ideals that have played so vital a role in the history of western nations. The ideas of democracy, individual worth, freedom in its various forms, the rights of man, divine purpose in the world, human destiny, and many other concepts of a similar nature, find their origin in part in the literature of the Old Testament. The influence of this book is also reflected in the great literatures of Europe and America. In fact the allusions to passages in the Old Testament are so frequent that many of the great books in English and American literature cannot be read intelligently without some familiarity with the context from which these passages have been taken.

To understand the writings that are included in the Old Testament one must bear in mind that they are predominantly an expression of the religious life of the ancient Hebrew people. It is in this respect that they must be distinguished from writings that are primarily scientific or historical in the secular sense in which these terms are used. Modern scientists and historians have as their main objective an accurate description of the way in which events have occurred. Whether these happenings are related to some divine purpose or merely illustrate the sequence of events it is not for them to say. They neither deny nor affirm any divine activity in what has taken place. This is not true of the Old Testament authors. They begin with the assumption of a divine being whose character and purpose are disclosed, at least to some extent, in the course of events. In harmony with this assumption, they write for the specific purpose of pointing out the divine element as they see it illustrated in the historical process. It is in this respect that the real significance of their writings is to be understood. It is a mistake to judge the value of the Old Testament account of events on the sole basis of either scientific or historical accuracy. Whether in these respects they are able to meet the requirements which are recognized today is beside the point. They were written with a different objective in mind. This does not mean that the narratives in the Old Testament have no historical value at all. They are recognized, even by secular historians, as one of the most reliable sources available for reconstructing the history of the Hebrew people. But as source materials they must be evaluated the same as any other source materials. The greatness of the writings lies in another area. It is to be found in the disclosure of the divine element in history along with the moral and religious lessons that are derived from it.

One further word should be added concerning the study of the Old Testament. This has to do with the concept of divine revelation. It has long been customary to regard the books of the Bible as the revealed word of God. There is justification for speaking of them in this way, provided of course that one understands the meaning of revelation. It is important to remember in this connection that revelation is always and necessarily a two-way process. It involves both a giving and a receiving. We may appropriately think of the giving as the divine element, and the receiving as the human element. However perfect the source of divine revelation may be, the human understanding of it is necessarily limited and subject to error. This is not to say that divine wisdom can never be imparted to human beings at all, but it does mean that the reception of this wisdom partakes of the limitations that belong to human understanding.

A SHORT OUTLINE OF OLD TESTAMENT HISTORY

To understand the Old Testament it is necessary to have some familiarity with the history of the people who wrote it. Judaism is a historical religion. This means that the ideas associated with it were disclosed to the Hebrew people through the concrete events which occurred in that part of the world where they lived during the centuries in which the Old Testament was in the making. A detailed account of the entire history of the Hebrew people would go far beyond the scope of these notes. A brief outline of some of the major high points in that history will be sufficient for our purpose.

While it is true that the books of the Old Testament begin with an account of the creation of the world, we must bear in mind that the narratives which deal with such topics as the creation, the Garden of Eden, the fall of man, the great flood, and other events related in the book of Genesis were never intended to be regarded as an accurate historical account of the entire world process. None of these accounts appeared in written form until some time after the Hebrews had become settled in the land of Canaan, west of the Jordan River, modern-day Israel. This did not take place prior to the ninth century B.C. Obviously, the stories which one finds in the early chapters of the book of Genesis as well as those which have to do with the activities of the patriarchs who were believed to have lived before the time of the exodus from Egypt were not written by eyewitnesses of the events which were recorded. Neither were they written by people who lived anywhere near the times about which they wrote. It was not until after the men who wrote had reflected on the events connected with the history of their people that any attempt was made to record these events or to set forth their meaning. When this was done, the interpretations necessarily reflected the perspective from which they were written.

The beginnings of Hebrew history are obscure and cannot be known with certainty. It is generally believed that the people from whom the Old Testament eventually emerged came from a group of Semitic tribes known as the Habiru. These tribes inhabited the region referred to as the Fertile Crescent, a strip of land lying between the Tigris and Euphrates rivers and stretching southward for some distance in the direction of Egypt and the Nile River. They are known to have moved about in this territory as early as 2000 B.C. Eventually some of these tribes migrated to Egypt and lived there for some time, probably three or four centuries. Apparently, they were at first welcomed by the Egyptians, for the Hebrew colony grew and prospered. In time their numbers increased to the extent that the Egyptians became alarmed lest their own security become endangered. In order to protect themselves against any further advances on the part of the Hebrews, the Egyptian Pharaoh inaugurated a program of harsh measures toward the newcomers, forcing them into a condition of servitude and slavery. This situation is the one referred to in the Old Testament as the period of Egyptian bondage. It was in connection with this period of oppression that we first learn of Moses and his role in bringing about the deliverance of his people. It was under his guidance and leadership that the Hebrews were able to leave the land of Egypt and journey to new territory where they were to make their home.

It was this exodus from the land of Egypt that marked the turning point in the history of the Hebrew people. It was the great crucial event that enabled them to become a separate nation. It was to this event that the great prophets and teachers of later generations always referred when they recounted the way in which their god—known to them as Yahweh—had dealt so graciously with them. The date usually given for the exodus from Egypt is about 1250 B.C. It was followed by a period of wandering in the wilderness, after which the various tribes now known as the Israelites established themselves in the land of Canaan. Those who had emerged from bondage in Egypt were then united with other tribes that had not been involved in the oppression, and together they formed the nucleus from which the Hebrew state came into existence.

Although the literature which is now included in the Old Testament did not begin to appear until after the settlement in the land of Canaan, it was only natural that the history of the people should be projected back into the period which preceded the migration into Egypt. The basis for doing this was the relatively large number of stories and legends which had been handed down orally from one generation to another. While there are good reasons for believing that these stories grew out of actual experiences, they cannot be regarded as authentic history, nor can we place the same reliance on them as we do on the accounts of events which occurred after the settlement in Canaan. Accordingly, it is customary among Biblical scholars to refer to the period which preceded the migration to Egypt as the age of the patriarchs, or the prehistoric era of the Hebrew people.

After leaving Egypt the Hebrews are said to have spent forty years wandering in the wilderness prior to their entrance into the land of Canaan. The number forty is generally understood to represent a relatively long period of time rather than an exact number of years. Although the settlement in Canaan is described in two widely differing accounts, we can be fairly certain that it required a considerable number of years before the invaders obtained full possession of the land. During this time the various tribes were organized into a confederacy, and judges were appointed to rule over the people. In theory at least, they were governed by Yahweh, who communicated directly with the judges. The theocracy came to an end when the people demanded a king and Saul was chosen to head the newly formed monarchy. He was succeeded by David and after David, Solomon became king. He was the last ruler of the united kingdom. After his death the kingdom was divided. Ten of the tribes revolted and formed what came to be known as the northern kingdom, or the Israelite nation. Because the tribe of Ephraim was the largest and most influential of the group, the new unit of government was frequently referred to as the Ephraimite kingdom. The two tribes which did not revolt became the southern, or Judean kingdom.

The two kingdoms continued until about the year 722 B.C., when the northern kingdom was overrun by the Assyrian empire. The people were taken into captivity and their national existence came to an end. The southern kingdom continued until 586 B.C., when it was conquered by the Babylonians and a large portion of the Hebrew people were forced to live in exile. The Babylonian exile lasted for more than a century, but it finally came to an end when permission was given to the Hebrews to return to their own land. They rebuilt the city of Jerusalem, restored the Temple and its services, and organized their state along lines that had been laid down by the prophets and priests of the exile. But the restored state never enjoyed the peace and prosperity which had been anticipated. Internal difficulties arose, the land was troubled with drouth and pestilence, and there was always the danger of attack from surrounding states.

The close of the Persian period and the death of Alexander the Great brought about a new set of circumstances most unfavorable to the Hebrews. Egypt and Syria were two rival powers each struggling for supremacy over the other, and the little Jewish nation became a buffer state between them. Toward the latter part of the second century B.C., the Maccabean war launched by Antiochus of Syria brought extreme suffering to the Jews and threatened complete destruction of their state. Fortunately, the Jews were able to survive this crisis. Under the leadership of Judas Maccabeus and his successors, they were able to regain the land which had been taken from them and become once again free and independent. This situation did not last very long. It was a troublesome period and one which finally terminated in the conquest of Palestine by the Roman government.

Some of the more important events and accomplishments in these successive periods of Hebrew history may be summarized briefly as follows:

The Prehistoric Period has to do with the stories and legends preserved by the Hebrews as a vital part of their cultural heritage. Narratives concerning the Hebrew ancestors enabled later generations to establish continuity with the great traditions of the past. To what extent these stories record actual events that took place we have no way of knowing, nor does it matter a great deal. The important thing about them is the way in which the ideals of a later age are reflected in them. Since the historical period of Hebrew activities begins with the exodus from Egypt, we can only say that the stories about what happened prior to that event is a record of what later generations believed to have taken place, although we do have good reasons for thinking these accounts were originally based on actual events. In these stories the beginnings of Hebrew history are traced back to Abraham. According to the record he was called out of the land of Ur of the Chaldeans, and to him it was promised that his seed should become a great nation and they would inherit the land of Canaan.

This promise seemed impossible of fulfillment because Abraham and his wife Sarah were both old and childless. However, God intervened and in due time Isaac was born. Isaac's two sons, Esau and Jacob, were the ancestors of the Edomites and the Israelites, respectively. Jacob's twelve sons were the progenitors of the twelve tribes of Israel. Because of a severe famine in Canaan, Jacob's sons went down to Egypt to buy food. One of the sons, Joseph, who had been sold into slavery at an earlier time, was now a prominent official in the Egyptian government. He had charge of the food supplies, and when his brothers came down to make their purchase they had to deal with him. His identity was concealed from them for a time, but eventually he made himself known. As a result of these meetings, it was arranged that Jacob as well as all of his sons and their families should move to Egypt where they were peaceably settled in the district known as Goshen. Here they remained until the Pharaoh of the oppression ascended the throne and began a policy of hostilities toward them.

The Wilderness Journey which followed the exodus from Egypt is marked by two important events that were closely related. One was the proclamation of a code of laws which, according to the tradition, Yahweh revealed to Moses on Mount Sinai. The other event was the establishment of a covenant, or contract, between Yahweh and the people of Israel. The basis of the covenant was the body of laws which Yahweh had given and which the people had agreed to obey. Yahweh's part of the contract consisted of his promise to care for them, supplying their needs and protecting them from the ravages or attacks that might be brought on by their enemies.

This covenant relationship between Yahweh and his people is one of the dominant ideas throughout the entire Old Testament. It served to distinguish Yahweh from the gods of the surrounding nations. These gods were, as a general rule, believed to be related to their peoples by the natural ties of physical descent. In other words, they were bound to their people by ties that were not dependent on any contractual agreement or on any type of moral qualifications. Consequently, they could not abandon their people because of any moral delinquency. But this was not true of Yahweh in his relation to the Hebrew people. His promise to remain as their god was conditional on their living up to the terms of the agreement. Whenever they failed to obey the laws he had given to them, he was no longer bound to protect them or even to claim them as his own people. The prophets of later generations would call attention to this fact and thus remind their contemporaries that security for the nation could not be expected so long as they failed to fulfill the requirements of the covenant to which they had been committed. This is no doubt one of the reasons why the religion of the Hebrews exhibits moral progress which surpassed that of the other nations.

The content of the law codes on which the covenent relationship was based is recorded in what is now known as the Book of the Covenant. It is found in Exodus 20:23-23:19. The famous decalogue, or Ten Commandments, which one finds in the first twenty-two verses of chapter 20 may have been included in the law code given by Moses, although we may be sure it was not given in the exact form in which we have it today. Tradition — both Jewish and Christian — has for many centuries regarded Moses as the great lawgiver of the Hebrew people. Accordingly, it has been held that he was the author of all the laws contained in the first five books of the Old Testament.

Modern scholarship has produced ample evidence to indicate that many of these laws were not known until long after Moses' own death. The fact that these same laws were attributed to Moses was not intended to deceive anyone concerning the time of their origin. Rather, it meant that these laws were in harmony with the ones given by Moses, and they were added for the purpose of continuing the work he had begun. How many of the laws contained in the five books known as the Pentateuch were actually given by Moses is not known. It is, however, reasonable to assume that the ones contained in the Book of the Covenant were first enunciated by him, since these laws are appropriate to the age in which he lived. The similarity of this law code to the older Babylonian code of Hammurabi has led many scholars to believe the Mosaic code was modeled after the Babylonian one. However this may be, there are unique elements in the Mosaic code and these may rightly be regarded as a distinctive Hebrew contribution.

The Settlement in Canaan is described in the books of Joshua and Judges. The accounts given were evidently derived from different sources, since there are significant differences between them. The conquest of Canaan required a considerable period of time and it was attended by some important changes in the daily lives of the Hebrew people. For one thing, it meant a change from a nomadic or shepherd type of living to a permanent settlement and an agricultural mode of securing a livelihood. This called for a new and different type of organization among the various tribes. It was for the purpose of bringing this about that a great assembly was called at Schechem. Under the leadership of Joshua steps were taken to unite the tribes into a kind of confederacy. It was an organization similar in many respects to what has been known in other cultures as an amphictyony. The new community thus formed was predominantly religious rather than political. Although membership in the community consisted mainly of

Hebrews, it was not limited by racial qualifications. Anyone who chose to worship Yahweh and who would promise to obey the laws he had given was accepted as a full member of the community. It was this body of people that came to be known as the twelve tribes of Israel.

The government of the new community was placed in the hands of individuals who were called "judges." These persons were believed to have received instructions directly from Yahweh, who communicated with them through dreams, visions, and other forms of charismatic experience. Deborah, for example, was one of these judges. She was the one who sent out a call to the scattered tribes to come to the aid of those who were being attacked by the Canaanites. The call was sent out in the name of Yahweh, whose intervention at a crucial moment enabled the Israelites to defeat their enemies in the battle which was fought on the plains of Megiddo. Gideon, whose little band of three hundred warriors achieved another important victory, was also a judge of Israel. Because of the success he had achieved, some of the people wanted to proclaim him king. Probably the chief reason for this was the felt need for a stronger type of organization to resist attacks being made by surrounding nations. Gideon refused to be king. However, after his death his son Abimelech yielded to the temptation, and an attempt was made to have him reign as king over Israel. The attempt failed but the demand for a monarchial type of government continued, and finally Samuel, who was the last of the judges, anointed Saul to be the first king of Israel.

The United Kingdom began with the reign of Saul and was continued under David and Solomon. Saul was in some respects an able ruler. He was a competent warrior and much of his time was spent battling the Philistines. His successes along this line won for him the praises and admiration of the people. He was not an arbitrary ruler but one who tried to follow the charismatic directions that had been in vogue during the period of the judges. During the latter part of his reign he was subject to prolonged periods of melancholy, which he interpreted to mean that the spirit of Yahweh no longer communicated with him. He was rebuked by the prophet Samuel for the way in which he conducted the war against the Amalekites, and his career ended in disaster when he died on the hills of Gilboa in the midst of conflict with the Philistines.

The reign of David marks the high point in the history of the united kingdom. He was regarded by later generations as Israel's greatest king. To be sure, he was idealized by the people who came after him and excuses were made for the unfortunate things that happened while he was king. Nevertheless, he was a great king and one who accomplished much for the nation he served. He succeeded in uniting the northern and southern tribes under one centralized government with headquarters at Jerusalem. He formulated plans for the building of a Temple and these were carried out after his son Solomon ascended the throne. David's reign was not altogether peaceful. It was marred by external conflict and internal dissension and revolt. In spite of these difficulties the nation grew and prospered. Centuries later no higher compliment could be bestowed on an Israelite king than to say he was like King David.

Solomon, too, was idealized by later generations but not in the same way as his father David. His greatest accomplishment was the building of the Temple at Jerusalem. In order to extend the power and influence of Israel among surrounding nations, he contracted a number of foreign marriages. The wives that he brought to Jerusalem were permitted to continue the worship of their native gods, and thus idolatry was introduced and encouraged alongside the worship of Yahweh. Solomon's building operations were made possible by heavy taxation, along with other burdens which the people were forced to bear. The resentment was so strong that when the question of who should succeed Solomon on the throne was raised, they inquired of Rehoboam about his attitude concerning the oppressive measures of his father Solomon. When Rehoboam replied that he would not only continue these policies but would be even more severe, ten of the tribes revolted and set up a new government of their own.

The Divided Kingdom began with the death of King Solomon and lasted until the fall of Samaria in 722 B.C., at which time the northern kingdom came to an end and the people were taken into captivity by the Assyrians. The southern kingdom continued until 586 B.C., when Jerusalem was destroyed and the Babylonian captivity began. The history of these two kingdoms is recorded in I and II Kings. The author evidently belonged to the southern kingdom, for his account indicates a strong bias in that direction. Concerning each of the kings who reigned in the north he uses the same statement: "This king did that which was evil in the sight of Yahweh." Some of the southern kings were evil too, but he was usually able to find some excuse for the things which they did. Since there was no fixed system of chronology for recording the dates when things happened, the events in the reign of each king were synchronized with what took place in the other kingdom.

The northern kingdom, known as Israel, had a very difficult time during the first century of its national existence. The tribes were frequently at war with neighboring states, and on more than one occasion peace was obtained only by making large concessions to the enemy. Later their fortunes changed, as they were able to regain most of what they had lost before. Under the leadership of King Jeroboam II, who reigned for more than half a century, Israel enjoyed a period of unprecedented prosperity. With the death of this king, a period of decline set in and conditions went from bad to worse. Moral decay led to political weakness and soon the nation became an easy prey for the advancing armies of the Assyrian empire. It was during the years which preceded the collapse of the northern kingdom that the prophets Elijah, Amos, and Hosea carried on their work.

The southern kingdom, known as Judah, lasted for more than a century after the fall of Israel. It occupied less territory than the northern kingdom and for the most part it led a more peaceful existence. All of the kings of Judah were direct descendants from the line of David, and this was of particular significance because it was believed that some day the Messiah would come from this line and under his leadership the full realization of the divine purpose in the history of the Hebrew people would be realized. The most prosperous period in the life of the southern kingdom came during the reign of Uzziah. After his death the country was invaded by the Assyrian army, and for a time it looked as though Judah would suffer the same fate that had come upon Israel. Then suddenly the Assyrian army withdrew and the nation was spared. But for the remainder of their existence as an independent nation the Judeans were forced to make concessions, including an enormous tribute to the Assyrian rulers. Likewise, after the fall of the Assyrian empire, they were subservient first to the Egyptians and later to the Babylonians. It was during the decline of the southern kingdom that many of the great prophets delivered their messages. These include Isaiah, Micah, Zephaniah, Jeremiah, Habakkuk, and others.

The Exile and After. When Jerusalem was captured by the armies of Nebuchadnezzar and the inhabitants of Judah were deported to Babylon, the worshipers of Yahweh were put to a severe test. To many of the people it must have appeared that the gods of Babylon had triumphed over the god of the Hebrews. If Yahweh still retained his power he must have forsaken his people, for they were now subject to a foreign power. The survival of the religion of the Hebrews in spite of these unfortunate circumstances was due in no small measure to the work of the two great prophets of the exile, Ezekiel and Deutero-Isaiah. They provided an interpretation of the captivity that was in harmony with their understanding of the nature of Yahweh, and they kept alive the hope of a return to their own land and the prospects for a glorious future of the restored state.

The captivity lasted for a long time. Eventually the Babylonian empire came to an end. It was overthrown by the Persians, who exhibited a more tolerant attitude toward the Jews. Cyrus, who was the head of the new empire, granted them permission to return to their own land. He even aided them in their preparations for the journey back to Palestine. But the return of the exiles did not prove to be the happy event which they had anticipated. They were disappointed in their efforts to rebuild what had been destroyed. They found their temple in ruins, the country was desolate; the land was plagued with drouth and pestilence; their neighbors were often hostile; and in many respects their lot was now more difficult than it had been while they were in captivity. Prophets offered their explanations for the way things were going and did their best to encourage the people to look for a brighter future. Priests were especially active and a new emphasis was given to the ritualistic aspect of their religion. Literary productions were numerous and legalism became the dominant note in the religion of Judaism.

Politically the affairs of the restored state grew steadily worse. The Persian empire ceased when it was overthrown by the Grecian armies under the leadership of Alexander the Great. His conquests included Palestine, along with the other countries which were brought under his control. He was tolerant of the Jews, allowing them to continue their religious activities so long as they did not interfere with his political ambitions. After his death conditions changed and the Jews experienced some of the most severe persecutions they had ever known, as Antiochus the ruler of Syria tried to obliterate completely the long established customs and traditions of the Jewish faith. This was the occasion of the Maccabean wars. When these wars were finally over the Jews did have a brief period of political independence, after which they became subjects of the Roman government.

THE CHRONOLOGICAL ORDER OF OLD TESTAMENT WRITINGS

The history of the Hebrew people is reflected in nearly all of the literature found in the Old Testament. Sometimes it is the history of the people as a whole, while at other times it is that of a smaller group or even the experiences of a particular individual. The makers of the Old Testament believed that Yahweh revealed himself through history in much the same way that we think a man's character is disclosed through his actions. It is for this reason that some familiarity with the historical setting of each of the writings is prerequisite to an understanding of them.

The exact order in which the contents of the Old Testament made their first appearance is not known. The literature as we have it today contains many fragments which appear to have existed separately at one time. They have been combined, copied, edited, supplemented, and arranged so many times that not even the most expert scholars are in complete agreement about the order in which they first appeared. This does not mean that we are unable to know anything about it, or that we cannot be reasonably certain concerning the approximate time when the various parts of the literature were produced. On the other hand, it does mean that our conclusions should be reached with considerable caution and we must always be ready to revise them in the light of new evidence. Our purpose here is merely to outline the approximate order of the writings in accordance with generally recognized Old Testament scholarship.

The Oldest Writings are now included as parts of historical narratives which did not reach their final form until a relatively late date. Many of them can be located with a fair degree of accuracy in the books of the Pentateuch, or first five books, of the Old Testament. Other early fragments may be found in the books of Joshua, Judges, and those portions of the Old Testament which deal with the early history of the Hebrew nation. Some of these writings are as old as the conquest of Canaan. It is quite possible that some of them are even older than that. Not all of the early literature of the Hebrews has been preserved in the Old Testament. We read, for example, of the "Book of the Wars of Yahweh," the "Book of Yashur the Upright," the "Book of the Acts of Solomon," the "Royal Annals," the "Temple Annals," and other documents. None of these have been preserved in their entirety but we know of their existence because of the Old Testament references to them. In several instances extracts have been taken from them and included in the later writings.

An exhaustive account of these early writings cannot be attempted here but their general character may be indicated by the following examples. Poems were written in commemoration of significant events. The "Song of Deborah" recorded in Judges 5 was one. It was written in celebration of a victory over the Canaanites. The "Fable of the Trees" found in Judges 9 had to do with the abortive attempt of Abimelech to become king over Israel. The "Blessing of Jacob," which is a part of Genesis 49, recalls Jacob's last meeting with his sons. The "Oracles of Balaam" recorded in Numbers 23-24 describe an experience which occurred during the wilderness march. "David's Lament" over the death of Saul and Jonathan is found in II Samuel 1:19-27 and a song celebrating a victory over the Amorites is recorded in Numbers 21:27-30. One of the oldest of these poems is Lamech's "Song of Revenge" found in Genesis 4:23-24. Miriam's "Song of Deliverance," Exodus 15:21, may be as old as the time of Moses.

Among the early narratives which were used as source materials for later histories were such documents as "The Story of the Founding of the Kingdom." It was written by an ardent admirer of King David and presents the story of his kingship in a most favorable light. He believed in the monarchy and describes in considerable detail the events that led to its establishment. He begins with an account of Israel's oppression by the Philistines because this shows clearly the need for a strong and capable leader. The prophet Samuel sees the proper qualifications in Saul and promptly anoints him to be the first king of Israel. He tells of important events in Saul's reign but the real hero of his story is David. The reader is impressed with the charm of David's personality as well as the accomplishments of his reign. Although he was proclaimed king at Hebron which was located in the south, he was able to win the loyalty and support of the northern tribes as well. As a means of further unification he made the city of Jerusalem, located midway between the north and south, the capital of the newly formed state. The story concludes with an account of the succession to the throne of David's son Solomon.

Two other narratives which furnished valuable information for later historians are the "Book of the Acts of Solomon" and the "Rise and Fall of the House of Omri." The first of these tells of King Solomon and the events which took place during the early years of his reign. His prayer at the dedication of the Temple, his request for wisdom to guide his people, and the grandeur of his building operations are given particular emphasis. The other narrative has to do with the reign of Omri, who was one of the more important rulers of the northern kingdom. Only parts of this narrative were used by the author of I Kings, for some of the material did not serve the purpose for which he wrote. The reign of Omri's son, King Ahab, is described at considerable length. The account is especially important, since it helps to correct some of the unfavorable impressions of this king conveyed by other narratives.

Stories concerning the work of the prophet Elijah and his successor Elisha are also a part of the early narratives produced in the northern kingdom. Of these stories which have been preserved, the ones having to do with Elijah are by far the most significant. They indicate a conception of Yahweh that is far in advance of ones previously held. The Elisha stories are indicative of a somewhat lower level of religious development. Their chief characteristic is a series of miracle stories. Strange and wondrous are the deeds said to have been performed by this marvelous miracle worker. They are presented as evidence of the favor and power of Yahweh.

No account of the early fragments which in time became parts of the Old Testament would be complete without mention of the laws which were designed to regulate human conduct. Probably the oldest of these laws are the ones contained in the Book of the Covenant. When they first appeared in written form we do not know. There are good reasons for believing these laws were known as early as the time of Moses, although they were probably not put in writing until a much later date. We do know that new laws were added from time to time as the need for them arose. Later, all of the laws were placed in the framework of history and, along with the early poems and narratives, were incorporated in the lengthy historical documents which constitute a relatively late but significant portion of the literature of the Old Testament.

The first books of the Old Testament to appear in the approximate form in which we have them today are the ones attributed to the *Prophets*. It would be a mistake to suppose that all of the contents found in the Old Testament books which bear the names of prophets were written by the persons for whom the books were named. Actually the work of the prophets themselves constitutes only the main basis or essential core of the books. Editors, copyists, and redactors added materials which they regarded as appropriate and these additions were preserved along with the original materials. The names of the prophetic books and the approximate order of their appearance may be indicated as follows. Amos and Hosea are the only ones which belong to the literature of the northern kingdom. Both of them were produced during the eighth century B.C. and they have to do with conditions which existed in Israel prior to the collapse of that nation. The books of Isaiah (1-39) and Micah come from the same century and they were addressed to the people of Judah, or the southern kingdom.

From the seventh century B.C., or the era which preceded the Babylonian captivity, we have the prophecies of Zephaniah, Nahum, Habakkuk, and Jeremiah. Of these four, the book of Jeremiah is not only the longest but also the most important. In many respects he has been regarded as the greatest of the Old Testament prophets. The books of Ezekiel and II Isaiah (40-55) are especially significant. They came out of the period of the exile and influenced to a great extent the development of religious ideals in the centuries which followed. The prophets of the post-exilic period are usually classified among the so-called minor prophets. The books in which their messages have been preserved are relatively small and their contents indicate they were men of lesser stature than the ones who appeared earlier. It is in this group that we have Haggai, Zechariah, Malachi, Joel, and Obadiah.

The Historical Writings which make up approximately one-third of the Old Testament cannot be dated or arranged as definitely or with the same degree of accuracy as the prophetic writings. The chief reason for this is the fact that they were in the process of being made over long periods of time. Whether they are to be regarded as early or late will depend on one's point of view. If we have in mind the source materials that were used, they are among the earliest of the writings. If we are thinking of the final form which the narratives assumed, they will be relatively late but not the latest of the writings to be included in the entire Old Testament. The historical books include the Pentateuch, or what is often referred to as the five books of Moses, and in addition, the books of Joshua, Judges, I and II Samuel, I and II Kings, I and II Chronicles, Ezra, and Nehemiah.

A complete analysis of the contents of these books is a very complex and difficult task. It is one concerning which there is no universal agreement among competent scholars. However, there are some conclusions which have found general and widespread acceptance. For example, few people would question that the Pentateuch is composed of documents written by different persons who were widely separated both in time and in point of view. The Graf-Wellhausen hypothesis of four separate and distinct narratives known respectively as J, E, D, and P, has been publicized for more than a century. Although many corrections and modifications have been made since it was first proposed, its main thesis still stands. Recent investigations merely indicate that the literature is even more complex and requires a larger number of documents to account for all the materials found in these books. In their final form the historical writings are presented in a manner which is designed to account for the laws and institutions peculiar to the Hebrew people from the time of creation to the post-exilic period. Thus we find the laws of Deuteronomy as well as those which belong to the so-called Holiness Code and the relatively late ones known as the Priests Code, included in historical narratives which attribute all of them to Moses. Obviously, one of the reasons for this was the added prestige which attaches to institutions when it is believed that they have been in existence for a long time.

During the post-exilic period it was considered necessary to attach great significance to those religious institutions which were unique among the Hebrew people and one of the most effective means for doing this was to indicate their ancient origin. Events belonging to the distant past were presented in a manner which would reflect the interpretation given to them at the times when the historical narratives were written. Thus we find the belief that the increasing sinfulness of man had shortened his life span reflected in the account of the large number of years the early patriarchs lived. And again the sordid events so numerous in the book of Judges reflect the sentiment of those who held that conditions which preceded the establishment of the monarchy were intolerable, since they permitted every man to "do that which was right in his own eyes."

The sacred writings of the Old Testament include not only the Prophets and the Historical Narratives but also a collection of Miscellaneous Books which are sometimes referred to as the *Hagiographa*. These writings cannot be dated with precise accuracy nor can they be placed in the exact chronological order in which they were produced. Concerning this group as a whole, it can be said they are relatively late and belong for the most part to the post-exilic period. Three of these books, Proverbs, Ecclesiastes, and Job, are known as *Wisdom Literature*. They are characterized by features which distinguish them sharply from the writings of the prophets. They are of international character and have to do with problems which are of a universal nature rather than those which were peculiar to the Hebrew people. Their appeal is to essential reasonableness instead of the "Thus saith Yahweh" of the prophets. The topics considered are ones which pertain to the practical affairs of everyday living.

The book of Daniel is one of the latest to be included in the Old Testament. It represents a different literary type which is known as *Apocalyptic*. As such it stands in sharp contrast with the prophetic writings. It was produced during a period of crisis which occurred in connection with the Maccabean wars. It was designed to strengthen and encourage those who were suffering extreme persecution. The book of Psalms is a collection of hymns, prayers, and poems reflecting both individual and group experiences of the Hebrew people from almost every period of their national history. A part of this collection was used as the hymn book of the restored Temple after the return from the Babylonian captivity. Short stories is an appropriate title for three books produced during the post-exilic years. They include Jonah, which is a classic protest against narrow-minded nationalism on the part of the Jews; Ruth, a delightful story written in protest against the law forbidding international marriages; and Esther, which provides an account of events leading to the origin of the feast of Purim. The book called Lamentations portrays some of the bitter experiences which followed King Zedekiah's flight from the city of Jerusalem at the time of the Babylonian conquest. The Song of Songs is a love poem which came to be included in the sacred writings because of the allegorical interpretation given to it.

SUMMARIES AND COMMENTARIES

THE PROPHETIC BOOKS

AMOS

Summary

The book of Amos consists of nine chapters. It is the earliest of the prophetic writings to be preserved in book form. Not all of the material found in these chapters came from the prophet himself. Editors and copyists added to the original oracles comments which they deemed appropriate in the light of events which had taken place after his death. Whether the words of Amos constitute a series of addresses or belong to one single address is not known. The theme which runs through all of them is one of protest against the social injustices which prevailed in northern Israel during the reign of Jeroboam II. Along with this protest is the warning that Yahweh will surely punish the nation for violating the demands of justice. The punishment will be nothing short of captivity by a foreign power and the end of Israel's national existence.

Amos was a shepherd who lived in the region of Tekoa, not many miles from the city of Jerusalem. He made his living by raising sheep and taking care of sycamore trees. When his produce was ready for market he would go to the towns and villages of Israel. His journeys would take him through the country districts, where he observed the hardships imposed on the working class of people by the wealthy landowners who lived in the towns or cities in the midst of comparative luxury. While in the cities he would be deeply impressed not only by the contrast between the rich and the poor but by the way in which the political and religious leaders tried to justify it. They insisted that Yahweh rewards in a material way those who are faithful in the performance of their ritualistic obligations to him. Hence they interpreted their own prosperity and that of the nation as a whole as evidence that the divine favor rested on them and would continue to do so for all time to come. At the same time they reasoned that the hard lot of the poor was exactly what they deserved, since they had not been regular participants in the sacrifices and other religious activities carried on at the established places of worship. Amos was not impressed by this kind of argument. He had been raised in an environment where it was understood that loyalty to Yahweh involved fair dealings among people rather than observance of religious rites and ceremonies.

As Amos pondered the situation which prevailed in northern Israel
he began to have dreams and visions. Three of these are recorded. In one
of them he sees a man with a plumb line measuring a wall that is about to
fall. He is told that the bulging wall is none other than the house of Israel,
and just as a wall of this kind will soon collapse, so the nation which it
represents will surely go into captivity. In a second vision he sees a basket
of summer fruit and this too represents the people of Israel. Their material
prosperity is like the fruit that is fully ripe. But ripe fruit lasts only a little
while and then it becomes rotten and decays. So the peaceful years of the
Israelite nation are about to come to an end. The third vision is one in which
he sees a swarm of locusts about to devour the produce of the land. This
vision is also interpreted as a warning of the evil day that lies ahead.

After a time Amos reaches the point where he can keep still no longer.
Addressing a group of people who had gathered at the place of worship
known as the Bethel sanctuary, he declared that Yahweh has this to say
to them:

I hate, I despise your feasts, and I take no delight in your solemn
assemblies. Even though you offer me your burnt offerings and cereal
offerings I will not accept them.... Take away from me the noise of
your songs. To the melody of your harps I will not listen. But let justice roll down like waters and righteousness like an everflowing stream.
Did you bring to me sacrifices and offerings during the forty years in
the wilderness, O house of Israel?

It was a daring statement for the prophet to make, since it was a direct
challenge to the generally accepted religious practices of the time. Strong
opposition developed at once when Amaziah the priest sent word to Jeroboam the king that Amos was a dangerous character and should be expelled
from the land. Although Amos insisted that he had spoken only the words
which Yahweh had told him to proclaim, Amaziah told him to leave the
country and never to prophesy again in the land of Israel.

The coming downfall and utter collapse of the northern kingdom is
the predominant theme of the book of Amos. The basis for this prediction
is not the rise in power of the Assyrian empire with its threat of invasion
from the north but rather the immorality expressed in the political, economic, and religious life of the nation. It was Amos' conviction that Yahweh
is a god of justice and his power over the nations of the earth is evidenced by
the fact that transgression of the principles of justice and social righteousness will inevitably be followed by ruin and decay. This is illustrated in the
first two chapters of the book which record oracles concerning Damascus,
Gaza, Tyre, Edom, Judah, and Israel. The first four of these tell of calamities

which have fallen upon the respective kingdoms and all because of their utter disregard for what was just and right. The last two indicate that both Judah and Israel are subject to the same kind of treatment.

Because they "sold the righteous for silver and the needy for a pair of shoes" and for the many other instances in which they have violated the principles of justice, the nation of Israel is doomed. The luxurious homes of the rich will be spoiled, the women who have spent their time in idleness and seeking for pleasure will be dragged away into exile, and the entire country will be laid waste. On this point Amos is especially emphatic. He insists that the coming captivity is a certainty and it will mean final and complete destruction. He declares "the virgin of Israel is fallen, and will never rise again." Whatever remnants may remain after the approaching invasion from the north will be insufficient for a rebuilding of the nation. They will be comparable to "a piece of an ear or a hind leg" which a shepherd may rescue from a sheep that has been torn to pieces by a lion or a bear.

The fate which is in store for Israel is fully deserved. The fact that their religious and political leaders have confidently believed that their manner of worshiping Yahweh would bring them continued peace and prosperity will avail them nothing at all. They have had the opportunity to learn from the experiences of the past that Yahweh's relationship to them is conditional on their obedience to his moral requirements. Because their opportunities in this respect have been greater than those of other nations, they must bear the greater responsibility. Yahweh is no longer obligated to protect them and he will not be influenced by their prayers, offerings, or solemn assemblies. This leads Amos to an interpretation of the "Day of Yahweh" that stands in sharp contrast to the one that had been generally accepted by the priests and other contemporary rulers of the land. In their opinion the coming of the Day of Yahweh would be a day of triumph and of gladness for the people of Israel. It would be a time when their enemies would have been subdued and their own peace and prosperity made permanently secure. This, they believed, would be the final realization of that divine purpose which from the very beginning had guided the destiny of Israel. But for Amos the coming of the Day of Yahweh could mean nothing of this kind. If Yahweh was indeed the god of justice, he could not show special favor to the Israelites by allowing them to escape the type of punishment which he had brought upon other peoples for exhibiting the same kind of conduct. The coming of the Day of Yahweh would, therefore, be a dark day for the Israelites. "Woe unto them that desire the day of Yahweh.... It is darkness and not light." The captivity of the nation would not mean the overthrowing of the god of Israel but rather the supremacy of the god of justice.

Commentary

The prophecies of Amos mark an important point in the development of the religion of the Old Testament. The prophet was indeed a "spokesman for Yahweh." That he was not speaking for himself or trying to please the ones who listened to him is made clear by the content of the message he delivered. Critics have often maintained that the Old Testament prophets created the god of whom they spoke out of their own imagination. Had they done so, it does not seem at all likely that Yahweh would have spoken so critically of what was being done by their own people.

It was customary in the ancient world for each nation to have its own god, a being whose power and influence would be limited by the boundaries of the country over which he presided. There is evidence to indicate that Yahweh had been so conceived by the Hebrew people. For Amos, Yahweh is not subject to these limitations. As a god of justice his demands are universal and consequently they affect all nations alike. Israel is no exception. Dishonesty and transgression of the rights of people will bring about the destruction of this nation just as surely as it has done so in the case of Tyre, Moab, Damascus, and Gaza. The implication is clear enough that Yahweh is the god of all nations. If Amos is not to be regarded as a pure monotheist, we can at least say that his thought is moving in that direction.

The opposition of the priests toward Amos can be understood in the light of what he had to say concerning the solemn assemblies, sacrifices, public prayers, and other ritualistic observances. It was the function of the priests to see to it that these activities were maintained, and Amos insists they are worthless and should be abolished entirely. This appears to be an extreme position, for ritual when it is used properly can be an aid toward spiritual ends. On the other hand when observance of ritual becomes a substitute for morality, nothing less than its total abolition would seem to be appropriate. This was undoubtedly the case with Amos.

There are several passages in the book of Amos, especially in the last chapter, which indicate that some day the Israelites will return from captivity and will be happy and prosperous in their own land. Whether these passages are from Amos or were added to the original by persons who lived at a later time is a question concerning which there is some difference of opinion. However, the weight of the evidence seems to indicate they are later additions. As the manuscripts were copied from time to time, it was inevitable that the message of Amos would be viewed from the perspective of later events, and it was only natural that insertions be made in order to bring the message into harmony with them. Furthermore the type of restoration which is indicated in the closing chapter of the book is not the kind which one would expect from Amos, since it indicates material prosperity rather than a moral transformation.

HOSEA
Summary

The book of Hosea contains fourteen chapters. Like the book of Amos, it is addressed to the people of the northern kingdom. It contains both a warning concerning events which lie ahead and an interpretation of their meaning. Throughout the book the prophet is speaking to the people of Israel about the critical situation which developed during the years that immediately followed the death of Jeroboam II. When Amos had prophesied concerning the disaster which would befall the nation, he was promptly repudiated by those who were "at ease in Zion" and who were confident that no evil would ever come upon their land. Only a few years later when Hosea came on the scene their attitude had changed. Events had taken place which were enough to shake the confidence of even the most optimistic persons. There was no longer any stable government on which the people could rely. The line of kings changed rapidly and often the change was attended by violence. Invasion by the Assyrian armies was imminent, and Israel was able to keep the peace only by paying an enormous tribute to the Assyrian rulers.

To raise this tribute it was necessary to impose a policy of taxation that placed a difficult burden on the people. There were always those who resented the paying of tribute to a foreign power. At times this resentment led to open revolt. The Israelite king would be murdered and his assassin would take over the reins of government. The situation was chaotic and no one seemed to know what to do. The priests in their desperation would increase the number of sacrifices, offer more prayers, and call more solemn assemblies, but none of these measures were able to stem the downward tide. It was under these strained and trying circumstances that Hosea performed his mission as a "spokesman for Yahweh."

The first part of the book of Hosea records the tragic story of the prophet's unhappy marital experiences. His wife, Gomer, whom he had married in good faith, proved to be an adulterous woman. Three children had been born but they were not Hosea's children. Because of her unfaithfulness it was necessary for the prophet to divorce his wife and live apart from her. Following her separation from the home, Gomer continued her adulterous life and eventually her lot was scarcely different from that of an ordinary slave. But Hosea still loved her in spite of her unfaithfulness. To rescue her from her paramours he sought her out and purchased her freedom by paying the price of a slave.

Whether this story is to be regarded as a parable or as the record of actual experiences in the prophet's home life is a question concerning which there are different opinions. The majority of Old Testament scholars believe it was the latter. This seems to be in accord with the materials found in the third chapter of the book, in which Hosea indicates clearly what he regards as the meaning of these experiences in relation to Yahweh's dealings with the people of Israel. The parallel is obvious. Yahweh had chosen Israel and entered into a covenant relationship with her. But Israel has been unfaithful to the covenant. She has forsaken the one to whom her loyalty was pledged and has gone away and served other gods. The licentious practices followed by the worshipers of the Canaanite Baal gods have become a part of the religious life of the Israelites, and even their professed worship of Yahweh has been contaminated with the ideas and ceremonial rites of Baal worship. Because of this unfaithfulness on the part of Israel, Yahweh will permit the Assyrians to overrun the land and carry the people into captivity. But unlike Amos — for whom the coming captivity would be final — Hosea looks upon it as a means for bringing the Israelites to their right senses. After they have learned their lesson, they will return to their own land and a king who is like unto King David will reign over them.

As this lesson which comes out of his own bitter marital experiences becomes clear to Hosea, he records it from the perspective of his later years. Seeing how his own relationship to Gomer parallels the relationship between Yahweh and Israel, he realizes that Yahweh has used this means to communicate his will and purpose to those who have claimed to be his own people. It is from this point of view that we can understand his statement that Yahweh had instructed him to marry an adulterous woman and again at a later time directed him to make provisions for her restoration.

The remainder of the book of Hosea consists of a miscellaneous collection of statements expressing his convictions concerning the character of Yahweh and his relation to the people of Israel. Hosea appears to have had the temperament of a poet and it is probably for this reason that his thoughts are usually expressed in terms of strong analogies and striking figures of speech. It is not always easy to understand what he is saying, for these statements, or perhaps we should say addresses, are not arranged in chronological order nor are we given any indication of the time or circumstances under which they were delivered. In spite of these difficulties, the materials contained in these chapters reveal some remarkable insights which contributed in no small way to the development of Israel's religious ideals.

As one reads the book of Hosea he is impressed first of all by the new element which is introduced in the conception of the deity. For Amos, as well as for most of his predecessors, Yahweh had been conceived primarily as a god of justice. It was believed that he had given laws for his people to obey, and disobedience of these laws must inevitably bring on punishment sufficient to atone for the wrongdoing. But for Hosea, Yahweh is primarily a god of love and mercy. Our best understanding of his nature can be grasped by means of analogies drawn from family relationships. The love of a husband for his wife and the love of a father for his children are appropriate symbols for indicating the character of the deity. Speaking for Yahweh, the prophet declares, "When Israel was a child I loved him, and called my son out of Egypt." And again, "How shall I give thee up Ephraim? How shall I cast thee off Israel? I will not execute the fierceness of mine anger. I will not return to destroy Ephraim." Punishment for wrongdoing is indeed necessary, but as Hosea sees it the purpose of punishment is not to meet the demands of justice but rather to restore the ones who have done the wrong. This is to be done by getting them to see for themselves the error of their ways and then in humility to repent and turn from their evil paths. In other words, for Hosea, punishment is remedial rather than retributive. Indeed, it is an expression of Yahweh's love for his people. It is something that is used as a kind of last resort to teach them lessons which they have refused to learn in any other way. Israel will surely go into captivity but it will not be a final or complete destruction of the nation. Rather, it will be an opportunity for them to gain a clearer understanding of the character of Yahweh so that when they return they will know how to worship him in an appropriate manner.

The responsibility for what has happened to the nation rests heavily on the priests. It was their function to guide the affairs of the nation, especially in regard to their religious duties. But this they have not done. They have been blind guides leading the people to believe that Yahweh demands nothing more than sacrifices, long prayers, solemn assemblies, and other forms of ritualistic observances. The truth of the matter, according to Hosea, is that Yahweh cares nothing at all for these services. "I desire mercy and not sacrifice, knowledge of God rather than burnt offerings." Yahweh's demands are moral. He desires the right inner attitudes rather than external conformity to a given set of rules. If the people had a correct understanding of the character of Yahweh they would not be trying to worship him after the manner in which the Canaanites had worshiped their Baal gods. It is for this lack of understanding on their part that Hosea criticizes not only the priests but the people who have allowed themselves to be misled in this manner. The Israelites have had the chance to know better and it is a part of their responsibility to make the proper use of the opportunities given to them. "My people are destroyed for lack of knowledge." "Because thou hast rejected knowledge, I will also reject thee."

Failure to understand the nature of Yahweh has led to false ideas concerning the safety and security of the nation. Instead of putting their trust in righteousness, they have relied upon strength and military power. When it became evident they could not match the strength of enemy nations who threatened to invade their land, there were those who advocated an alliance with some foreign power. One group urged an alliance with Egypt while another one insisted that the security of Israel was dependent on an alliance with Assyria. Hosea was convinced that both parties were wrong. He accused Israel's leaders of failure to understand the true cause of the downfall of the nation. "Ephraim," says the prophet, "is like a cake that is not turned." They are a half-baked lot who do not have any clear idea of what they are doing. Again, he says, "Israel is like a silly dove." They resemble a bird that is without brains. They have been following a stupid policy, trying to save their country by making it strong instead of making it morally right.

Commentary

Hosea was the last of the prophets of the northern kingdom. Fortunately, the book which bears his name has been preserved. When the Assyrians overran the land, someone escaped to the south and brought the manuscript with him to the city of Jerusalem. It is an important document for it represents in some respects the highest achievements in the development of the religious ideals of Israel. It is here that we find for the first time the conception of Yahweh as a god of love. Earlier notions had placed the emphasis on power and justice as the essential characteristics of the deity. Hosea does not eliminate these qualities but he does make them subordinate to love and mercy. The way in which he arrived at this new conception is of particular interest. We would infer from the account given in the first three chapters of the book that it came to him partly as a result of his own experiences. While in one sense it was a revelation from Yahweh, we must bear in mind that even a divine revelation can be communicated to human beings only through the use of finite channels. It is true that a perfect understanding of the nature of deity is beyond any human capacity. Nevertheless, it is possible to know something about it, provided there is any similarity or resemblance between the human and the divine. On this assumption it is reasonable to suppose that the most adequate conception of deity will be derived from those experiences which are regarded as the noblest and best human beings have ever observed in their own lives.

This is what seems to have happened in the case of Hosea. The attitude which he had displayed toward Gomer in spite of her unfaithfulness to him and the efforts which he had put forth to bring about her restoration were recognized at a later time as the noblest and best of all that he had ever

30

done. In view of this fact, it was only fitting that he should think of Yahweh as one who possessed in an even greater measure those qualities of character that were similar to the best he had experienced in his own life. From this it would follow that Yahweh's attitude toward the erring people of Israel would be like that which he had displayed toward Gomer. His main concern with reference to them would be that of bringing about their restoration rather than meting out to them the exact amount of punishment which they deserved. In other words, Yahweh's justice is always subordinate to his mercy. Justice in human relationships is based on the idea of equality, which means giving to each person exactly that which is his due. As Hosea sees it, divine justice is determined not so much by what people deserve as it is by what is necessary in order to bring about the desired reformation on their part.

This new element in the conception of deity had many important consequences for the future development of Israel's religion. For one thing, it meant that Yahweh's punishments could be interpreted as remedial rather than retributive. From this point of view the entire history of the Hebrew people would appear in a new light. It would mean that the hardships and tragedies which had befallen them from time to time were for the purpose of teaching them lessons which they had refused to learn in any other way. Even the captivity of the nation by a foreign power would not mean that Yahweh had forsaken them. His love for the Israelites was so strong that he would never give them up. It was true that Israel had been slow in learning the lessons these experiences were designed to teach, but now that the light was beginning to break through there was at least some hope for the future. Eventually the divine purpose with reference to Israel would be fully realized.

ISAIAH
Summary

The book of Isaiah as it now appears in our Old Testament contains far more than can be attributed to the first prophet who bore that name. The book as a whole is a rather large collection of writings that were produced by a number of different authors, some of whom were separated by relatively long periods of time. For example, it has long been recognized by Old Testament scholars that chapters 1-39 constitute a unit that is quite separate and distinct from the one found in chapters 40-66. It is the former that has usually been attributed to the prophet Isaiah, since it deals primarily with Judah and Jerusalem at a time when the city was still standing and the southern kingdom was threatened with invasion by the Assyrians.

The second unit, which begins with chapter 40, appears to have been written from the point of view of conditions which prevailed more than a century later. In fact the author indicates very clearly that the Babylonian captivity has been in existence for a long time. He believes that the punishment is about over and the time is near at hand when the captives will return to the homeland and rebuild the city of Jerusalem, which has long been in ruins. A careful reading of each of these two units of the book reveals further that the prophet Isaiah did not write all of the first thirty-nine chapters, nor did one person write all that is contained in chapters 40-66. There is ample evidence to indicate the work of several different authors. The editors who finally assembled the entire collection of manuscripts placed them all under the name of Isaiah, since they were quite certain of those materials which belonged to him, and putting them all together would indicate their location in the sacred writings rather than precise authorship of each part.

Isaiah was a prophet of the southern kingdom. His call to the prophetic office took place in the year that King Uzziah died. It was a critical period in the history of the nation. Uzziah had been one of Judah's greatest kings. He had reigned for approximately half a century, and during this time the kingdom had enjoyed its greatest period of prosperity. Commercial relations had been established with neighboring states and the internal resources of the country had been developed. However, this increase in wealth and the way in which it was distributed had brought about some serious problems. The contrast between the rich and the poor had reached an alarming state, which brought threats of a revolt from those who had been deprived of their lands and other possessions. Then, too, there was an added threat from without, for the advance of the Assyrians against northern Israel was an indication that the time was not far distant when Judah might expect an invasion from that same quarter. The situation was indeed ominous, but because Uzziah had been a strong and able ruler the people had confidence that he would know how to deal with these problems. Then came the startling news that the king had leprosy and would have to leave Jerusalem and live in a leper colony outside the city. His son Jotham, who was the next heir to the throne, possessed none of the strong and admirable qualities which were characteristic of his father. Instead, he was a weak and vascillating person quite unable to inspire confidence on the part of his subjects. Uzziah lived for three years in the leper colony. The news of his death brought shock and consternation to the entire kingdom.

It was at this time and under these critical circumstances that Isaiah became a prophet. The vision which he interpreted as his call to service is recorded in chapter 6 of the book of Isaiah. The scene in which the vision occurred is the Temple in the city of Jerusalem. It was here that the religious life of the nation was centered and it was to this place that Isaiah, a young man probably in his early twenties, turned in an hour when the future of his country looked especially dark. The vision is described in considerable detail. The essential meaning of it is expressed in the prophet's deep conviction that in spite of Judah's dark hour Yahweh was still in control of the nations. His glory and majesty filled the whole earth. The contrast between Yahweh's holiness and the sinful state into which the Judean kingdom had fallen was something that called for immediate action. Someone must speak for Yahweh and communicate the divine message to the people. Knowing what a difficult task this would be, Isaiah pleads that he is quite unfitted to perform it. Then an act takes place which symbolizes an inner cleansing of his heart and mind after which he responds to the call with the words "Here am I, Lord, send me."

Isaiah's ministry lasted over a period of approximately half a century. It continued through the reigns of Jotham, Ahaz, and Hezekiah. Tradition tells us that he suffered a martyr's death during the reign of King Manasseh. His work brought him into direct contact with kings and priests, and he encountered strong opposition from each of them. At times this opposition was so strong that he was forced to give up speaking in public and confine his ministry to a group of disciples with whom he would meet privately. With regard to the priests and the services which they performed, Isaiah expressed convictions that were similar to those spoken to the people of Israel by Amos and Hosea. For example, we hear him saying "Of what use is the multitude of your sacrifices to me, says the Lord." And again, "Your new moons and your appointed feasts my soul hateth." He even insists that Yahweh will not listen to their prayers. "And when ye spread forth your hands, I will hide mine eyes from you." "When ye make many prayers, I will not hear: your hands are full of blood."

In the same spirit Isaiah criticizes the economic policies that were not only sanctioned but encouraged by the rulers of the land. In the "Song of the Vineyard," which was probably chanted by the prophet, we find these words, "Woe unto them that join house to house and add field to field, till there be no place that they may be placed alone in the midst of the earth." This was a protest against the way in which the poor people were deprived of their property in order to satisfy the claims of their creditors, who had taken unfair advantages of their unfortunate circumstances in order to enrich themselves.

The prophet's criticism of the king was expressed on many occasions but on none of them was it more pronounced than when he protested against the foreign alliances that were being negotiated. Early in Isaiah's ministry, he warned King Ahaz against the dangers involved in an alliance with

Assyria. The heads of the two puppet kingdoms which were all that remained of northern Israel had asked King Ahaz to join with them in a coalition against Assyria. When Ahaz refused they threatened to make war against him. Ahaz was frightened and wanted to appeal to Assyria for help. Isaiah saw clearly the folly that would be involved in a move of this kind and in a prophecy which has often been misinterpreted as a reference to a coming Messiah, he warned King Ahaz that within three or four years at the most those two kingdoms that he feared would be completely routed. On the other hand if he wanted to do something that would really be a protection for Judah, he should give his attention to those conditions which were in need of a moral reformation. The king did not heed Isaiah's advice. He went ahead with his plans and as a result Judah was placed in a subservient relation to the Assyrian empire. During the reign of King Hezekiah, on two different occasions, an attempt was made to curb the rising power of the Assyrians by forming alliances that would resist any further advances on their part. The first of these was promoted by the Egyptians, who invited the Judean king to join with them. The second one was initiated by Merodach-baladin of Babylon, who visited king Hezekiah and tried to persuade him to have Judah join with the Babylonians and the Egyptians in a united front against Assyria. King Hezekiah, fearful that Judah would be unable to stand alone, was inclined to join the alliance. Isaiah knew that it would be a grave mistake for him to do so. In one of the strongest messages which he delivered to the king the prophet declared, "Woe unto them that go down to Egypt for help; and stay on horses, and trust in chariots. Now the Egyptians are men and not God, and their horses flesh and not spirit." "When the Lord stretches out his hand, the helper will stumble, and he who is helped will fall, and they will all perish together."

In spite of the immediate dangers which the nation of Judah faced, Isaiah was confident of the ultimate triumph of the Hebrew people. Like Hosea, who had looked on the approaching captivity of northern Israel as merely a prelude to a reformed and triumphant Hebrew society, Isaiah was sure that any temporary disaster would not be the final end of the Judean kingdom. Yahweh's purpose in the world was to be realized through the Hebrew people, and this meant for Isaiah that the city of Jerusalem and that for which it stood could never be completely overthrown. When the Assyrian army did invade Judah, capturing thirty-five fenced cities and demanding of Hezekiah that he surrender the city of Jerusalem, Isaiah advised the king not to yield to their demands. He insisted that Jerusalem was Zion's city and it would never fall. Within a short time the Assyrian army withdrew and for at least a brief period Isaiah was vindicated.

Closely related to Isaiah's teaching concerning the "surviving remnant" that would be the hope of Judah were his predictions with reference to the coming of a Messiah, or "anointed one," who would someday occupy the throne in Jerusalem and rule the nation with justice and righteousness. He will be a far better king than any of those who have preceded him. Under his leadership the poor and the oppressed will find a champion, for he will judge their cases with a discerning mind and will not be unduly influenced by hearsay or mere outward appearances. His kingdom will be the fulfillment and realization of the divine purpose in the world.

Commentary

Israel's messianic hope, though implicit in the teachings of some of the earlier prophets, finds its first clear expression in the prophecies of Isaiah. The term means "anointed one," or one who has been chosen by Yahweh for the accomplishment of a specific purpose. Among the Hebrews, kings and priests as well as prophets were usually anointed by a special ceremony which would symbolize their dedication to the work for which they had been called. When Saul was chosen to be the first king of Israel he was anointed by Samuel, and this ceremony symbolized the hope of the people that under his leadership the nation would realize its chosen destiny. But Saul did not measure up to these expectations and the same was true of all the kings that had followed in the line of succession of King David. The man who succeeded King Uzziah was notoriously weak and incompetent. It was then that Isaiah centered his attention on the coming of a Messiah who would possess the good qualities that had been so lacking in the actual kings. In one prophecy he is portrayed as an ideal king, while in another one he is characterized as an ideal judge who will understand the problems of the poor and the oppressed. He will see to it that their rights are protected and that they are given their just dues. During the centuries which followed the career of Isaiah, the concept of a coming Messiah took on a number of different meanings. In time it became one of the most important characteristics of Judaism.

One of the best known passages in the book of Isaiah is recorded in chapter 2 and deals with the subject of the coming of a warless world. Looking into the distant future the author envisages a time when the nations will "beat their swords into plowshares and their spears into pruning hooks. Nations will not lift up their swords against nations, neither shall they learn war any more." This prophecy, like the one recorded in chapter 35 where "the wolf and the lamb shall lie down together" and "they shall not hurt nor destroy in all my holy mountain," seems to be an admirable supplement to the idea of a coming Messiah who will be know as "Prince of Peace," and for this reason both of these passages have often been attributed to Isaiah. However, the evidence indicates very strongly that these prophecies come from a later period. The same is true of several of the oracles concerning foreign nations, especially the ones having to do with the destruction of Babylon and the future regeneration of the Assyrian nation. The fact that these oracles were finally included in the collection of Isaiah's own works is an indication of the high esteem with which they were regarded.

MICAH

Summary

The prophet Micah was a contemporary of Isaiah. He lived in a little village called Moresheth not far from the city of Gath which was destroyed by the Assyrians when they invaded Judah. Living in this small village, he came into daily contact with the people who suffered most from the system of land tenure against which Isaiah had protested. When he began his ministry the northern kingdom was still standing, and Micah's earlier messages were addressed to the people of Israel as well as to those living in Judah. Micah lived among the poor people and sympathized with them because of their hard lot. In many respects his work was similar to that of the prophet Amos. This is especially true with regard to what he had to say about social and economic conditions. While there is little if anything that is new in his criticism of the ruling classes, the manner in which he spoke caused his name to be remembered and honored among the prophets and teachers of later generations.

No writer in the entire Old Testament was ever more indignant than Micah over the ways in which the rich and powerful used every opportunity to exploit the poor and the weak. In deep earnestness he cried out: "Woe to them that devise wickedness and work evil upon their beds! When the morning dawns they perform it, because it is in the power of their hands." He denounced with bitterness the wealthy landowners because "they covet fields and seize them; and houses and take them away: they oppress a man and his house, a man and his inheritance." He characterizes the way in which the poor and the unfortunate have been treated as no better than that which is accorded to animals. Using the most forceful language, he denounces those "who tear the skin from off my people....and break their bones in pieces, and chop them up like meat in a kettle."

Because of these evil conditions Micah tells his hearers that Yahweh will surely bring punishment on the land. The captivity of the northern kingdom by the Assyrians was the punishment visited upon them because of their iniquities, and the prophet now sees a similar fate in store for Judah. Unlike Isaiah, who had boldly proclaimed that the city of Jerusalem was Zion's city and for that reason it could never fall, Micah could see no justice in having it spared. Because it was the capital of the nation and the home of the ones who were most responsible for the corrupt practices which prevailed in the land, it was they who deserved punishment even more than those who lived in the country villages where they were the victims of these unfair practices. For these reasons Micah proclaims in bold words: "Hear this you heads of the house of Jacob....who build Zion with blood, and Jerusalem with wrong. Because of you Zion shall be plowed as a field; Jerusalem shall become a heap of ruins."

Micah's warnings were resented on the part of those who preferred to hear that all was well and no evil would come upon the land. He knew that his messages were not the kind that would gain popular approval but true to his calling as a prophet he declared, "But as for me, I am filled with power, and with the spirit of the Lord, and with justice and might, to declare to Jacob his transgression and to Israel his sin." Whether Micah believed that the judgments on Israel and Judah would be the final end of these nations as Amos had taught, or believed they would be preparatory to a redeemed society as Hosea had taught, we do not know. Hope for the future is expressed in the one messianic prophecy which is recorded in chapter 5, but whether this is the word of Micah or an addition to the book made by a later writer we cannot be certain. The unique thing about this prophecy is that it names Bethlehem as the place where the Messiah will be born. This indicates a belief that the coming Messiah will be a representative of the poorer classes of people and understanding their situation he will champion their cause.

Commentary

Although there are seven chapters in the book of Micah, it is highly probable that only the first three can be attributed to the prophet Micah. He is usually classified with the minor prophets, but his work was evidently held in high esteem by later prophets and teachers. References to him were made on several occasions and his writings have been preserved along with some of the choicest materials to be found in the entire Old Testament. For example, the prophecy concerning the coming of a warless world found at the beginning of chapter 4 is quoted more frequently than any other portion of the book. It is identical with the one found in chapter 2 of the book of Isaiah. The original author is not known, but it is significant that the editors of each of these two books valued it so highly that they included it in each of their collections of writings.

Another notable passage in the book of Micah is the one found in 6:6-8. It is here that one finds a clear statement of prophetic religion at its best. "What doth Yahweh require of thee, but to do justly and to love mercy and to walk humbly with thy God." The author of these words understands that Yahweh desires moral qualities on the part of his worshipers rather than sacrifices and burnt offerings. It is doubtful if one could find in the religious literature of any people a more exalted conception of the nature of true religion and the moral qualities it is designed to promote.

ZEPHANIAH, NAHUM, AND HABAKKUK

Summary

Not all of Israel's prophets were men of great vision. Some of them apparently made little or o impression on either their contemporaries or their successors, with the result that neither their names nor their writings have been recorded. The three who are included in this section were more fortunate for we do know their names, and at least a part of what they had to say has been preserved in the books which bear their names. But as in the case of the other prophets, their messages are now combined with additions and editorial comments made by those who brought the manuscripts into their present form.

Zephaniah's ministry occurred during the reign of Josiah, king of Judah. We are told that he was the grandson of Hezekiah, but we cannot be sure it was the same Hezekiah who ruled in Jerusalem during the times of Isaiah. Zephaniah was in the true sense of the word a prophet of doom. He saw no bright future in store for his people. He is remembered primarily for what he had to say concerning the coming of the Day of Yahweh. "I will utterly consume all things from off the land.... I will consume man and beast..., and I will cut off man from off the land, saith the Lord." It is generally assumed that the immediate occasion which brought forth this prediction was a threatened invasion of the land of Judah by the Scythians, a barbarian horde that had been sweeping across neighboring countries with unparalleled devastation and destruction. We do know that an invasion by the Scythians did occur about this time but whether the prophet had them in mind or the Assyrians, who had long been the oppressors of the Hebrew people, we do not know. In either case he believed that events which would soon take place should be interpreted as the judgment of Yahweh being visited upon Judah because of her sins. He mentions specifically the worship of foreign gods on the housetops and the observance of ceremonies that were customary in connection with their worship.

Although Zephaniah was not the first prophet to predict the coming of the Day of Yahweh, he gave to this concept a specific meaning that was new to the people of his time. Amos had proclaimed that the Day of Yahweh would come sometime, but Zephaniah declared that it was already imminent. "The great day of the Lord is near, near and hastening fast.... A day of wrath is that day, a day of distress and anguish." He sees its coming as a great climactic event when the forces of evil will receive their just punishment. Whether he regarded this evil day as the termination of the Judean kingdom or viewed it as a necessary prelude to something better for his people we do not know. Some parts of the book of Zephaniah do predict the coming of a better day, but it seems quite probable that these were added by editors who looked at the book as a whole from the perspective of later years.

The book of Nahum is usually classified with the minor prophets. We know practically nothing about him as a person. From the contents of the book we would judge that he was not a prophet in the true sense of the word. He was a poet who possessed a remarkable style of writing and who described the fall of Nineveh, the capital of the Assyrian empire, in unforgettable language. Nineveh fell in 612 B.C. The event was an occasion for rejoicing on the part of the Jews, especially those in whom the spirit of nationalism was strong. The original poem is recorded in chapters 2 and 3. The first chapter contains an acrostic poem, which is used as an introduction to the book. It is possible that the author of the main poem may have witnessed the battle which brought destruction to the city, but of this we cannot be sure. The poem opens with a series of denunciations. These are followed by a vivid account of the capture of the city, and it concludes with a list of sarcastic remarks about a power that has boasted so much and is now laid low. For all of its remarkable qualities as an example of poetry, it is really a hymn of hate. For centuries the Hebrew people had suffered at the hands of the Assyrians and in the light of those bitter experiences we can see why this poem appealed to the editors who included it along with the writings of the prophets.

The book of Habakkuk reveals a spirit that is in sharp contrast with Nahum. The prophet for whom the book was named does not express hatred toward foreigners nor does he pronounce doom upon the evildoers among his own people. Instead, he is deeply disturbed over the course that events have taken, and he prays earnestly for light that will help him to understand the situation which prevails. His ministry occurred during the reign of Josiah and that of his son King Jehoiakim. Josiah is usually regarded as one of the better kings of Judah. It was during his reign that the famous law book was discovered in the Temple and its provisions were made the law of the land. In spite of all his good deeds, Josiah was slain in the battle of Megiddo, where he had gone to stop the advance of the Egyptians across Judean territory. His son Jehoahaz was taken in captivity to Egypt and another son, Jehoiakim, was allowed to occupy the Judean throne only because he pledged loyalty to the Egyptians. Later, when the Egyptians were defeated by the Babylonians at the battle of Carchemish, Jehoiakim switched to the other side and pledged loyalty to the Babylonians. In the meantime his attitude toward the people over whom he ruled was anything other than honorable.

As Habakkuk observed these happenings he could not understand why the evil forces in the world should prosper as they were doing. He had believed that Yahweh was a just god who rewarded the righteous and punished the wicked. But the events which he had observed seemed to indicate just the opposite. Josiah the good king had been killed in battle. His son who was the rightful heir to the throne was in captivity and Jehoiakim, who now ruled in Jerusalem, was a corrupt and incompetent king. The longer his reign continued the worse the situation became. The prophet could not understand why Yahweh didn't do something about it. In desperation he cried out: "O Lord, how long shall I cry for help, and thou wilt not hear?... So the law is slacked and justice never goes forth. For the wicked surround the righteous, so justice goes forth perverted." He has been told the Babylonians are an instrument which Yahweh is using to punish the evildoers in Judah, but it seems to him the instrument in this case is no better than the ones who are punished. This causes him to inquire, "Why dost thou look on faithless men, and art silent when the wicked swallows up the man more righteous than he?" Although Habakkuk does not receive a direct answer to his inquiry, he does find consolation in the assurance that someday the forces of righteousness will be triumphant and in the meantime "the just man shall live by his faith."

Commentary

The problem which troubled Habakkuk became even more acute during the centuries which followed. The teaching of the earlier prophets that the calamities which befell a nation should be regarded as punishments for their sins was questioned more and more in the light of observed experiences. The strong, powerful nations were not more righteous than the ones that were subservient to them. Within the nation, it was often the righteous person who suffered the most unjust treatment while the wicked person enjoyed comforts and prosperity. No final solution to the problem was ever found, but Habakkuk's statement that "the just man shall live by his faith" has inspired some of the most important movements in religious history.

The book of Nahum, which describes in exquisite language the fall of the city of Nineveh, contains no lofty religious sentiments. Its inclusion in the Old Testament has sometimes led to various interpretations of the imagery used in the poem. When these expressions are given a symbolic rather than a literal meaning, it is possible to read into the poem whatever one wishes to find. However, interpretations of this kind are legitimate only when the context indicates that the author intended it to be used that way. In the case of Nahum's poem, there is no indication that he is talking about anything other than the destruction of the city which had been responsible for so many of the woes inflicted on the Hebrew people.

Zephaniah's references to the coming of the Day of Yahweh anticipated in some respects the development of the eschatological and apocalyptic ideas that were destined to play so important a role in the centuries which preceded the beginning of the Christian era. Because the concept of a just god who was supreme over the nations of the earth implied the giving of rewards and punishments commensurate with the deeds of the people, the question of when and how all of this would take place was bound to receive more and more attention on the part of prophets and teachers.

JEREMIAH
Summary

The book of Jeremiah is the largest of the prophetic books of the Old Testament with the single exception of the book of Isaiah, which, as we have noted, contains the works of more than one prophet. In the book of Jeremiah we find that in addition to the prophet's own words there is a considerable amount of material of a biographical and historical nature. This material is especially valuable, since it reveals the personality of the prophet more clearly than this is done in any of the other prophetic books, and furthermore it provides information concerning the more important events in Jeremiah's career. The influence of this prophet's life and teachings had a profound effect on the future development of both Judaism and Christianity. In the New Testament there are many indications that both Jesus and Paul not only accepted certain of Jeremiah's ideas, but they gave to them a central place in their own interpretations of the meaning of religion. For this reason, along with others, Jeremiah has often been regarded as the greatest of the Hebrew prophets.

The period in which Jeremiah lived and worked was one of the most critical in Hebrew history. His public ministry began during the reign of King Josiah and lasted until sometime after the fall of Jerusalem and the beginning of the Babylonian captivity. He encountered strong opposition from kings Jehoiakim and Zedekiah, and on more than one occasion his life was threatened. After the fall of Jerusalem he was permitted by the Babylonians to remain in his homeland, while many of his fellow countrymen were taken into captivity. Some time later he was taken to Egypt quite against his will by a group of exiles who found it necessary to flee there for their own safety. It was here that the prophet died after a long and troublesome career.

The collection of writings which make up our present book of Jeremiah includes oracles, addresses, prayers, and exhortations, all of which were spoken by the prophet himself. These are arranged without any reference to either topical or chronological order. They are interspersed with materials which, though relevent to Jeremiah's work, were contributed by other persons. We shall attempt only a brief summary of the more important ideas set forth in Jeremiah's teachings.

The book begins with an account of his call to the work of a prophet. The account is written from the perspective of his later years, when it seems clear to him that even before he was born Yahweh had a plan or purpose for him to fulfill. His earliest prophecies, like those of Zephaniah, are believed to have been concerned with the threatened invasion of Judah by the Scythians. He believed his country would be completely devastated and that this would be a proper punishment for the sins which they had committed. The fact that his predictions in this respect were not fulfilled was seized upon by his critics as evidence that he was a false prophet.

One of the important events which took place a few years after Jeremiah began his prophetic work was the discovery of the law book in the Temple at Jerusalem. This book, which included the main part of what we now call the book of Deuteronomy, was declared to be the word of Yahweh, and King Josiah made it a part of the law of the land. Jeremiah was for a time enthusiastic about this move on the part of the king, for obviously the laws were intended not only to correct many of the social injustices which prevailed in the land but also to protect the worship of Yahweh from contamination with the evil influences of heathen forms of worship. It was hoped, and apparently with good reasons, that the enforcement of these laws would bring about a great and sorely needed reformation. Jeremiah observed the situation both before and after the new laws were introduced. He became convinced that the conduct of the people was no better under these laws than it had been before. This observation led to some very important consequences in his conception of religion and its purpose in the life of the Hebrew people.

The reason for the failure of the Deuteronomic reformation was not to be found in the character of the laws but rather in the motives which were dominant in the lives of the people. The prophet's conception of human nature is well expressed in the statements which he made. "The heart of man is deceitful above all things, and desperately wicked." "Can the Ethiopian change his skin or the leopard his spots? No more can ye do good who are accustomed to do evil." Man is so constituted that he follows his desires rather than his intellect, and for this reason he cannot change from his evil ways until there has been a change of heart. Furthermore, it was his conviction that man cannot by himself change his own nature. This can be brought about only through cooperation with Yahweh, and Yahweh can act on human hearts only when they recognize their need for it. But without this inner transformation in human nature all reformative movements are destined to fail.

After leaving his home town of Anathoth to live in the city of Jerusalem, Jeremiah experienced continual opposition from both the political and the religious leaders of Judah. The occasion which prompted some of this opposition was an address — or perhaps a series of addresses — concerning the Temple and the services which were being conducted in it. Because of the formal character of these services and their failure to change the inner lives of the people, Jeremiah saw that something very drastic would have to be done in order to bring people to their senses. They were putting their trust in the Temple, feeling certain that so long as it remained in their midst no evil could befall them. To get them to see that the true meaning of religion consists in a change from within rather than conformity to external requirements it would be necessary to take away from them the external objects in which they had placed their trust. Therefore, the prophet declared, the day is coming when the Temple will be destroyed. The ark of the covenant will be taken away, and even the nation that has called itself the chosen of Yahweh will be taken into captivity. These statements aroused the anger of the priests and those who were closely associated with the king.

Jeremiah was charged with treason and he would probably have been put to death had not some of his friends succeeded in hiding him until the wrath of his enemies had subsided. When it was no longer considered safe for him to appear in public, Jeremiah dictated a series of oracles in which the policies of the king and his subordinates were severely criticized and warnings were given concerning what would happen if these were not changed. When the scroll on which these oracles were written was finished, it was sent by a messenger who saw to it that the document was read aloud in the presence of the king. King Jehoiakim was displeased as he listened to the reading. Taking the scroll from the reader he cut it into shreds with his penknife and threw it into the fire. When news of what the king had done reached Jeremiah, he dictated the entire scroll over again, adding a specific warning to the king, and sent the new copy back to be read again.

Nothing that Jeremiah taught during his entire career was of more significance than his doctrine concerning the new covenant. In chapter 31 we read: "Behold the days are coming, says the Lord, when I will make a new covenant with the house of Israel and the house of Judah." The old covenant was based on the laws which had been given as far back as the time of Moses. It was a contract or agreement between Yahweh and the Israelites, in which the people had agreed to obey all of the commandments that had been given to them. But the Israelites had not lived up to the terms of that agreement, and now Jeremiah believed that he knew the principal reason why they had not done so. It was because of the evil desires and wrong motives that were a part of their nature. The only thing that could bring about a right relationship with Yahweh would be a change of heart, or in other words, a new nature. This was not something they could bring about by themselves but under the new covenant Yahweh promises to do for them that which they cannot do for themselves. Speaking for Yahweh Jeremiah declares, "I will put my laws within them, and I will write it upon their hearts; and I will be their God, and they shall be my people." He concludes by saying that when this is done it will no longer be necessary for specific rules to be given in order that people may know what they ought to do. With a changed nature and the right desires present within him, each person will know what is the right thing to do in any situation that arises.

Closely associated with this conception of the new covenant was the teaching of the prophet concerning individual responsibility. The prophets who had preceded Jeremiah usually spoke in terms of a social solidarity, which meant that Yahweh's relationship to Israel had to do with the nation as a whole. It was the entire group that would be judged and either punished or rewarded. One of the Ten Commandments had referred to the iniquities of the fathers being visited upon the children even to the third and fourth generations. When the people of Judah responded to Jeremiah's warnings of impending disaster by saying they were being punished not because of their own sins but because of the sins of their ancestors, he challenged this ancient doctrine. He declared that each individual would be held accountable for his own conduct. "In those days they shall no longer say 'the fathers have eaten sour grapes and the children's teeth are set on edge.'"

Commentary

The inwardness of religion in contrast with mere external forms of worship may be regarded as the dominant theme in all of Jeremiah's teachings. For him the relationship between the individual and his God was the most essential element in genuine religious experience. The external forms of worship, such as the offering of sacrifices, payment of vows, and participation in the services carried on in the Temple, were meaningless except insofar as they might contribute toward a changed nature in which Yahweh's spirit would take possession of one's mind and heart. The prophet believed that even the Babylonian captivity was being used by Yahweh as a means for bringing the Israelite people to a full realization of the fact that their God could be worshiped in a strange land without any of the external factors associated with the Temple in Jerusalem. In a foreign land they would learn that true religion is a matter of the heart and it can be experienced by any individual who establishes a right relationship between himself and the deity. This was indeed a lofty conception of religion and one that was far above the level on which the majority of the people lived. Conformity to external requirements is always an easier course to follow, and during the centuries which followed, it was the ritualistic element in religious practices which received the greater emphasis. Nevertheless, Jeremiah's conception was never completely lost. There were always some who adhered to it and from time to time new teachers would arise and give to his view a renewed emphasis.

In spite of Jeremiah's pessimism with reference to the immediate future of the Judean kingdom, he never abandoned the hope that eventually the divine purpose would be realized by his own people and in their own land. Throughout the book of Jeremiah, predictions of impending disasters are usually followed by the words "Nevertheless, I will not make a full end." This hope was symbolized by his action when he bought a piece of land that had belonged to the ancestral home. He took pains to see that the deed was properly recorded, even though he was well aware of the fact that captivity was close at hand.

Jeremiah's own religious life is revealed to a considerable extent in the prayers which are recorded. They illustrate in a unique way the intimate relationship which existed between the prophet and the deity whom he worshiped. They are usually in the form of conversations and they are characterized by a sincerity and frankness that is seldom found in one's prayers. He simply opened his mind and heart to Yahweh and did not hesitate to state whatever he felt to be the truth. If he thought Yahweh had been unjust in dealing with him he expressed his complaints in clear and unmistakable terms. But his prayers were never monologues in which he did all of the talking. After he had spoken he would listen for Yahweh's response and the entire conversation would have a significance for him that went far beyond the more formal type of prayer. It was the personal honesty of the man, as well as his courage and remarkable insights, that has caused later generations to think of him with admiration and esteem.

EZEKIEL
Summary

The book of Ezekiel has the most logical arrangement of any of the prophetic books. It contains three sections and each of these has a definite

45

subject matter of its own. The first one, which includes chapters 1-24, has to do with the fall of the city of Jerusalem. The third section, which consists of chapters 40-48, presents a plan for the rebuilding of the Temple and reorganization of the restored state of Israel. Chapters 25-39 contain a series of oracles addressed to the foreign nation, concluding with a section in which the future of Israel is contrasted with that of the foreign nations.

Ezekiel was one of the younger men taken to Babylon in the first captivity, which occurred in 597 B.C. He served as a kind of pastor to the Hebrew exiles who were allowed to live in a colony by themselves near the banks of the river Chebar. It is generally assumed that the most of what is contained in the book of Ezekiel was written by the prophet himself. For some time it was believed he wrote practically the entire book while living in the colony of exiles. Recent scholarship has, however, pointed out several reasons for thinking that at least a portion of the chapters included in the first section contain speeches delivered by the prophet in person to the people who remained in Jerusalem until the city fell in 586 B.C.

The book opens with an account of the vision which summoned Ezekiel to the prophetic office. A detailed description is given of an elaborate and complex image which symbolized the majesty of Yahweh and proclaimed his sovereignty over all the nations of earth. The prophet was so overcome by the vision that he fell on his face. A voice called to him saying, "Son of man, I send thee to the children of Israel, to a rebellious nation that hath rebelled against me...and they, whether they will hear, or whether they will forbear, yet shall know that there hath been a prophet among them." Ezekiel is then handed a scroll, "and there was written therein lamentations, and mourning and woe." He was told to eat the scroll and when he did so he found that in his mouth it was sweet as honey. Evidently he knew that the message he was to proclaim was one of impending disaster, and yet he thoroughly enjoyed the task that was given to him.

The people who were left in Jerusalem after the first captivity consoled themselves with the idea that they were better than the ones who had been taken to Babylon. They believed Yahweh would protect them from any foreign power and that neither the city of Jerusalem nor the Judean kingdom would ever be overthrown. It was Ezekiel's task to disillusion them with reference to this hope. He must make clear to them not only that the city would be destroyed but also the reasons why it would be overthrown. To accomplish this task the prophet performed a number of symbolic acts. He drew on a piece of tile a picture of the city of Jerusalem under siege and placed the tile in a prominent place where it could be seen plainly by all those who walked along the street. He laid on his left side for a period of time each day for three hundred and ninety days, and then he laid on his right side in a similar manner for forty days. To those who would inquire what it all meant, he would explain that for each day he laid on his left side northern Israel would be in captivity for one year, and for each day he laid on his right side the southern kingdom, or Judah, would spend a year in captivity. He cut off his hair, dividing it into three parts, which symbolized northern Israel, the Judeans left in Jerusalem, and those who were in captivity in Babylon. He rationed his food, carried furniture out of his house, and did various other things to represent the disaster which would soon overtake the city of Jerusalem.

The reason for the captivities that had already taken place as well as the one in store for the people left in Jerusalem was defiance of Yahweh's laws. Because Ezekiel believed Yahweh was supreme over all the nations of the earth, any violation of his commands without appropriate punishment would constitute an infringement upon his honor. This was a serious matter for Ezekiel, evidenced by the fact that his references to punishments are usually followed by the words "To the end that they may know that I am Yahweh."

It was because of her sins that Jerusalem must be destroyed. In his enumeration of these sins Ezekiel includes both moral and ceremonial transgressions, but it is noticeable that he placed the greater emphasis on matters pertaining to the ritual. He condemns most of all the worship of idols which represent foreign deities. He has severe censure for those who eat forbidden meat or violate any of the other rules having to do with the conduct of worship. Coming into direct contact with that which is unclean was one of the ways in which Yahweh's sanctuary would be contaminated and his holy name profaned. This was something that Yahweh would not tolerate.

Ezekiel, no less than Jeremiah, saw the significance of the individual in his relationship to Yahweh. Rejecting the idea that fathers may be punished for the sins of their sons or the sons punished for the sins of their fathers, he states boldly that it is the soul that sins that shall die. Furthermore, he appears to carry this idea to the extreme position of maintaining that one's entire life will be judged in terms of his last act. Concerning the man who has lived wickedly all of his life but before he dies turns from his wickedness and does that which is lawful and right, all of his wickedness will not be remembered. He will be judged as a righteous man. The reverse will be true of the man who has lived righteously all of his life but turns to wickedness just before he dies. All of his righteousness will not be remembered.

The fall of the city of Jerusalem presented something of a problem, especially to those who believed that Yahweh's presence in the most holy place in the Temple was a sure guarantee that the place would never be overthrown. They remembered Isaiah's words uttered more than a century before when he declared that Jerusalem was Zion's city and it must stand forever. For Jeremiah these words meant very little, since for him Yahweh's dwelling place was in human hearts rather than a specific place in the Temple. While this idea was not entirely absent with Ezekiel he, nevertheless, believed there was a sense in which Yahweh's presence was located in the Temple more than in any other place. How then could the Temple be destroyed so long as Yahweh's presence was in it? Ezekiel answers this question by saying that Yahweh's presence went up out of the Temple and rested on a hill outside. It was after this had happened that the building fell.

In the section dealing with the foreign nations, Ezekiel has one predominant message. These nations are subject to Yahweh's laws the same as the Hebrew people. The fact that they have not recognized his sovereignty will not alter their fate in the least. In the end they will be destroyed. This will take place in order that "they may know that I am Yahweh." Although Yahweh is, in Ezekiel's mind, a universal God, this does not mean that he stands in the same relationship to the foreign nations as he does to the people of Israel. In this respect Ezekiel's views are decidedly nationalistic. Yahweh punishes the Israelites in order to teach them a lesson which they have refused to learn in any other way. But in the case of the foreign nations, the purpose of the punishment is not to teach them a lesson that will bring about their conversion. With them the coming destruction is to be final and there is no anticipation of any reformation on their part. With reference to the Israelites, something quite different will happen. Yahweh will transform their character by putting his own spirit into their hearts. This restoration will include those from the northern kingdom as well as the people of Judah. In the vision of the valley of dry bones, the prophet proclaims a complete restoration of the whole house of Israel. They will go back to their own land, rebuild the kingdom that was overthrown, and Yahweh will dwell in their midst forever. The final destruction of all the foreign nations is described as an event that will take place when their vast armies under the leadership of Gog and Magog attempt to capture the restored city of Jerusalem. At the crucial moment when it appears that victory is in sight for them, Yahweh will intervene and completely destroy all of their forces.

The last eight chapters of the book of Ezekiel contain a description of the restored state as it is envisaged by the prophet. The Temple is to be built outside the main part of the city and constructed in a manner that will make it possible to keep out all of those persons and objects which might contaminate the holy place in which Yahweh will dwell in their midst. A sharp distinction is introduced between priests and Levites in order that only qualified persons should enter the building even for the purpose of keeping it clean. The highest official will no longer be the king but rather the high priest, thus indicating that political affairs shall always be made subordinate to religious considerations.

Commentary

Ezekiel has often been called the father of Judaism. His influence on the future development of Israel's religion was, at least for several centuries, greater than that of any of the other prophets. His conception of holiness, which stands in sharp contrast to that of Isaiah, became dominant in the period which followed the return from the Babylonian exile. For Ezekiel holiness was a quality present in things as well as in people. Holy objects would be profaned whenever anything common or unclean was brought into direct contact with them. This led to a sharp distinction between the secular and the holy and gave a new meaning to such items as the observance of dietary laws, payment of tithes, and observance of the Sabbath day. Violation of any of these rules would constitute a profanation of that which was holy or sacred. This interpretation of rules and regulations which were peculiar to the Israelite religion served to strengthen the spirit of nationalism and thus to increase the antagonism which already existed between Jews and non-Jews.

Ezekiel's conception of the final triumph of the Israelite people over all of their enemies and the complete destruction of the foreign nations contributed much toward the development of the eschatological doctrines which played so prominent a part in the religion of post-exilic Judaism. The idea that the whole human race is divided into two classes, known as the righteous and the wicked, and that the righteous can be identified as the ones who are living in strict conformity with all of Yahweh's laws, while the wicked are those who do not obey these laws, was but a further development of the teachings of Ezekiel. It is true that this position was not accepted by all of the post-exilic Jews. In fact some parts of the Old Testament were written for the specific purpose of refuting it. Nevertheless, it was a doctrine which appealed to the larger number of persons and served to characterize in a general way the attitude of late Judaism.

Ezekiel's plans for the rebuilding of the Temple and the reorganization of the state were carried out to a considerable extent when the exiles returned to their own land. It was the High Priest rather than a king who assumed the greatest responsibility in political as well as in religious affairs. The use of foreign slaves or common servants to do the menial tasks in the Temple was discontinued and only those who belonged to the tribe of Levi were permitted to enter the building for this purpose. In earlier times the entire tribe was regarded as having been set apart for the priest-hood, but now only a select group within this tribe were allowed to officiate in the services of the Temple.

The spirit of Ezekiel's work determined to a very great extent the char-acter of the religious life of the people during the centuries which followed. It can be seen in the code of laws known as the Holiness Code, which one finds in Leviticus, chapters 17-26, and again in the lengthy and detailed set of laws known as the Priests Code, which is now regarded as one of the four main narratives included in the Pentateuch.

DEUTERO-ISAIAH

Summary

Chapters 40-55 of the book of Isaiah are believed to be the work of a prophet who lived with the Hebrew exiles during the Babylonian captivity. He is usually designated as the second or Deutero-Isaiah, since his real name is unknown and his work has been preserved in the collection of writ-ings which included the prophecies of the earlier Isaiah. The chapters which are attributed to this prophet of the exile include some of the noblest of the religious ideals to be found in the entire Old Testament. The prophet was a pure monotheist. Rejecting the idea of Yahweh as a god who belonged primarily to the Hebrews, he boldly proclaimed him to be the only true God of the entire universe. He maintained the so-called gods of the foreign nations were but figments of the imagination. His conception of the people of Israel was also unique in that he regarded them as "the servants of Yah-weh" whose primary function in the world was that of carrying true religion to the ends of the earth. He made explicit an interpretation of history which though it had been implied in the teachings of the earlier prophets had never been stated as clearly by any of them. Finally, he introduced a new concept to account for the sufferings of people which could not in all fairness be explained as punishment for their sins.

The task which this prophet faced was that of giving new hope and encouragement to the exiles, who were on the verge of despair, feeling either that Yahweh had forsaken them entirely or that his power had been broken by the superior gods of the Babylonians. To these disheartened people Deutero-Isaiah calls out, "Behold your God!" He assures them that Yahweh has not forsaken his people and neither has he been defeated by the Babylonians or any other foreign power. He is the supreme ruler of the universe and all the nations of the earth are subject to him. "Behold, the nations are like a drop from a bucket, and are accounted as the dust on the scales." And again, "All the nations are as nothing before him, they are accounted by him as less than nothing and emptiness." He heaps ridicule on those who bow down before idols which have been fashioned by men's hands. It is not sufficient for them to say that these idols are but representations of their gods. The only true God cannot be represented or symbolized by an image, since there are no objects in nature to which he can be compared. Yahweh is the creator of the heavens and the earth. Whatever exists is dependent on him. He alone has the power to create and he is the only being whose purpose can be discerned in the course of history. "It is he who sits above the circle of the earth, and its inhabitants are like grasshoppers." "It is he who brings to nought and makes the rulers of the earth as nothing."

To those who have grown weary of the captivity and who have despaired that the time would ever come when they could go back to their homeland, the prophet has a message of comfort and of hope. He tells them the time has arrived when their warfare is over and their punishment is accomplished. It is Yahweh who declares that already they have been punished too much. He has called Cyrus, the Persian king, to take appropriate steps for their liberation and their return. Yahweh is now ready to lead them himself. He will go before them, making the rough places smooth and gently carrying in his bosom the ones who are unable to travel by themselves.

Yahweh's sovereignty over the nations of the earth is illustrated in Deutero-Isaiah's conception of history. Men and nations may think they have complete control over the course of events but in this they are mistaken. There is an order which characterizes the historical process. Although this order is moral rather than mechanical and allows for choice on the part of human beings, it is nevertheless a kind of order which establishes a relationship between antecedent and consequent which remains constant. It is this constancy which forms the basis for predictions. It is in this connection that Yahweh's power and foreknowledge cannot be matched by any of the gods of the foreign nations. Speaking on this point the prophet says, "Remember the former things of old, for I am God and there is none other; declaring the end from the beginning and from ancient times things that are not yet done, saying my counsel shall stand and I will accomplish all of my purpose."

In a series of poems called "Songs of the Suffering Servant," the prophet sets forth his greatest contribution to Israel's religious ideals. It is here that he points out the purpose and the opportunity that lie behind the unmerited suffering on the part of comparatively innocent persons. The problem which troubled Habakkuk had become one of the major issues for the exiles in Babylon. Granted that they had made many mistakes, they had not been as unjust or as wicked as the nations to which they had been made captives. If suffering is to be interpreted as punishment for sins, it ought to be distributed on a different basis than what they had experienced and observed. Deutero-Isaiah does not deny that at times suffering may be a just punishment for sins, but he does insist that not all suffering may be interpreted this way. Having in mind the captivity of the Israelite people, he is able to see in it something more than punishment for the mistakes they have made. He sees it as an opportunity to do something generous and noble for the benefit of those who have held them in captivity. Instead of suffering for their own sins, he sees in the experience the possibility of a voluntary suffering because of the sins of others. This could be the means of winning over their enemies to a new way of living which would be in harmony with the principles of justice and righteousness.

This was indeed a new way in which they might find at least a partial explanation for the suffering and hardships which they had experienced. Looking at it this way, it would be possible to see the realization of a divine purpose through the course that events had taken. The prophet sees the Israelite people as Yahweh's servants. It was true they were the chosen people but chosen for the task of suffering in order that true religion might be brought to those who could be reached in no other way. What could not be accomplished by force or argument might be achieved through the power of love as manifested in the voluntary suffering of the innocent for the sake of the guilty. Speaking for Yahweh the prophet says, "Behold my servant, whom I uphold...I will put my spirit upon him, he will bring forth justice to the nations." After identifying the servant with the people of Israel and Judah he says, "It is too light a thing that you should be my servant to raise up the tribes of Jacob and to restore the preserved of Israel; I will give you as a light to the nations that my salvation may reach to the end of the earth."

Commentary

No prophet of the Old Testament ever reached loftier heights in his understanding of religion than did Deutero-Isaiah. In his conception of Yahweh as the creator of the heavens and the earth, he made a sharp distinction between Yahweh and the deities of the foreign nations. Yahweh was the being on which all existence was dependent. He could not be adequately conceived as like any of the objects in the created universe. It is true that the prophet speaks of Yahweh as a person, for if the deity is to have any meaning for human beings it must be conceived in terms that have been drawn from experience, and personality is the most appropriate symbol that can be found. This does not mean that Yahweh is like human personality in every respect but only in some of them.

His interpretation of history is a recognition of the fact that the course of events is something more than a chaotic sequence without any meaning or order. It means that there is a divine as well as a human element in history, and in consequence of this there is a purpose to be achieved through the historical process. This is what the prophet means when he declares that Yahweh knows the end from the beginning. His predictions do not imply that all the things which happen are known in advance nor do they imply that human beings cannot alter the course of events by the choices which they make.

The greatest achievement of Deutero-Isaiah was his development of the idea of vicarious suffering. Although he was speaking primarily about the suffering of his own people, we must not think he was attempting to give a historical account of the way they were responding to their misfortunes. Rather, he was setting forth an ideal, which if it were to be followed, would throw new light on the question of unmerited suffering. It would enable the people to realize that the situation in which they had been placed provided an opportunity for them to exhibit to the foreign nations the true spirit of their religion. Like the other prophets before him, Deutero-Isaiah never doubted that the divine purpose would ultimately be achieved, but the method by which it would be accomplished was in his judgment something quite different from what had been conceived before. Vicarious suffering was an idea of great significance, and although it seems to have been too lofty an ideal for the majority of the people either to grasp or to follow, there were always some who appreciated its truth. Through the centuries which followed there were many occasions in which this ideal was exemplified. Christians have long recognized that in the life and death of Jesus of Nazareth we have a supreme example of what the prophet proclaimed to his contemporary exiles in Babylon.

THE POST-EXILIC PROPHETS
Summary

Prophecy in the Old Testament reached its greatest heights during and preceding the Babylonian exile. Jeremiah, Ezekiel, and the two Isaiahs were the men who made the most profound impressions on the religious development of the Israelite people. The period which followed the exile saw the work of a number of prophets, some of whom produced writings that have been preserved in the Old Testament, but in general they were men of limited vision and consequently their work was not on as high a plane as that of the prophets we have just named. To be sure there were some exceptions. The literature which belongs to this period contains some of the best insights to be found in any of the prophetic writings, although in most instances the authors of these passages are unknown. We will treat in this section only those prophets for whom books in the Old Testament were named.

Haggai. When the exiles came back from Babylon they experienced many bitter disappointments. Both Ezekiel and Deutero-Isaiah had promised so much that the people expected an era of great happiness and material prosperity. But it did not turn out that way. In spite of the help and encouragement given them by Cyrus, the Persian ruler, when they got back to their own land they found conditions in a miserable plight. The land had been neglected, the buildings were in a dilapidated state, the people who had remained had become careless and indifferent toward their religious obligations, and there were other difficulties. To make matters worse, the neighboring states assumed a hostile attitude toward the Hebrews so that in attempting to rebuild the walls of their city it was necessary to have their swords close at hand while working with bricks and mortar. It was under these conditions that Haggai appeared as a spokesman for Yahweh.

His message was essentially one of reproof because the people had neglected to build a Temple so that Yahweh might dwell in their midst. In this we see exemplified the spirit of Ezekiel's teachings. The people responded to Haggai's message and set to work with a will. They were handicapped by lack of means and materials but they did the best they could under the circumstances. When they had finished, the prophet told them that even though the building they had erected was poor in comparison with the earlier Temple, Yahweh would be with them and in due time the promises he had made would be fully realized.

Zechariah joined with Haggai in bringing a message of hope and encouragement to those who had returned from the exile. His analysis of the situation was more profound than that of his contemporary. He realized that something more than a rebuilding of the Temple was necessary before Israel's hopes could be realized. A moral transformation must take place within the people themselves. They must be cleansed of the evil elements in their own natures. Furthermore, the foreign nations whom they considered as their enemies would have to be subdued, but this could not be done by the Israelites taking up arms against them. It would be accomplished by Yahweh when the time was ready for him to act.

Zechariah's messages were expressed in a series of eight visions, each one of which symbolized some aspect of the situation having to do with the future of the people. In one of these visions the prophet sees an angelic surveyor measuring the area on which Jerusalem is to be built and marking the line of the wall. The interpreting angel explains that the city will have no need of a wall because Yahweh's protection is all that will be needed. In another vision Joshua the high priest stands before the angel of Yahweh in soiled clothes. At his right stands Satan, the accuser, who brings charges against Joshua and the people to whom he ministers. The angel does not accept these accusations. Joshua is then clothed with a white robe, symbolizing the fact that the sins of the people have been forgiven. Other visions symbolize the destruction of the forces of evil. One of the most significant statements to be found in the book is the one in which the message of Yahweh comes to Zerubbabel saying, "not by might, nor by power, but by my spirit, saith the Lord of hosts."

Malachi. Another prophet whose name we do not know spoke to the returned exiles offering them an explanation of the situation which they faced. He is known as Malachi not because this was his name but because the word means "messenger," and in his predictions concerning the future he had said that a messenger would precede the coming of the day of Yahweh and would prepare the people for it. Later editors supposed erroneously that the prophet was referring to himself, and hence this name was attached to his writings. He was not a great prophet, but he did have some words of encouragement as well as rebuke for the people to whom he addressed his messages. He insisted that Yahweh still loved the Israelites in spite of all the misfortunes that had befallen them. As evidence of his concern for them Malachi called attention to the fact that the Edomites had been severely punished. This was good news to the Israelites, for they had come to despise the Edomites as traitors to those whom they should have befriended. Now that a terrible catastrophe had been visited upon them, the prophet quotes Yahweh as saying, "yet I loved Jacob, but Esau I hated, and made his mountain a desolation."

There were reasons, too, why Yahweh had for so long a time withheld his blessings from the Israelites. One of these was their frequent use of sick and inferior animals for sacrificial offerings. Yahweh demanded the best and would be satisfied with nothing less. Another reason why Yahweh did not bless them was their failure in the matter of tithes and offerings. Here the prophet accuses them of robbing God. Again there were those who had divorced wives of their own people in order to marry daughters of foreign ancestry, and this was contrary to the will of Yahweh. So careless and indifferent had many of the people become, that the prophet could say that even among the Gentiles Yahweh's name was honored and feared more than it was among them. When the Israelites repent and correct all of these mistakes, Yahweh will open the windows of heaven and pour out a blessing so great that the people will not be able to receive all of it. This blessing, the prophet tells them, will include such material benefits as bountiful crops, increase of their flocks, and freedom from sickness.

Obadiah is another unknown prophet whose work has been preserved in a book which contains a single chapter. Usually works of this length were placed in larger collections of manuscripts and included under the name of a different author. Presumably in this case it was believed that the work would attract more attention if placed by itself. The book is the least significant both from the literary and the religious points of view of all the prophetic writings. It is decidedly nationalistic in tone. In the first part of the chapter, rejoicing is expressed over the fall of the Edomites. The remaining portion predicts the triumph of the Hebrew people at a time when all of their enemies will be destroyed.

Joel. Nothing is known concerning the life of this prophet. There is some lack of agreement concerning the time when he lived but this is not a matter of great importance. The book opens with the description of an unusually severe plague of locusts. This is followed by instruction in which the priests are told to proclaim a fast and to call a solemn assembly. The purpose of the meeting is to arouse the people to the need for repentance and reformation. They must "rend their hearts and not their garments." When this has been done Yahweh will pour out his spirit on all flesh, causing their sons and daughters to prophesy, their young men to see visions, and their old men to dream dreams. This will be a prelude to the coming of the great day of Yahweh when his kingdom will be established on the earth.

Commentary

The prophets of this period are of particular interest because they indicate the various trends of thought that were taking shape during the centuries which followed immediately after the return of the exiles from Babylon. The Temple in Jerusalem and the many ceremonies and activities associated with it came to occupy a most important place in the religious life of the people. This is especially true in the case of Haggai, for he believed Yahweh's presence as well as his blessings were dependent upon a proper place in which he might dwell in their midst. The distinction between the secular and the sacred was emphasized by Malachi. It is also implied in the work of other prophets, and as time went on it came to occupy more and more attention on the part of the priests. The spirit of nationalism, which in some instances reached the point of hatred toward Israel's enemies, can be seen in Obadiah and to a lesser extent in Joel and some of the other writers.

It would, however, be a mistake to suppose these tendencies were present in all of the prophetic writers. Voices were heard from time to time in which the spirit of Jeremiah and of Deutero-Isaiah found magnificent expression. We do not know the persons who possessed these voices, but many of their messages have been preserved in the later chapters of the book of Isaiah. The introduction of the figure of Satan in the prophecies of Zechariah, as well as the eschatalogical implications of his series of visions, marks an important trend in the development of post-exilic Judaism.

THE HISTORICAL WRITINGS

Approximately one-third of the Old Testament consists of historical documents. These include the Pentateuch, or what has often been called the five books of Moses, and in addition to these, the books of Joshua, Judges, Samuel, Kings, Chronicles, Ezra, and Nehemiah. When all of these writings are taken together, they may be regarded as covering the high points in the history of the Hebrew people from the time of the exodus from Egypt to the post-exilic period. In addition they are presumed to cover important events pertaining to the same people from the creation of the world to the time of the Egyptian bondage. The Hebrew prophets were especially concerned with history because they believed it was through the course of events that Yahweh's nature and will were revealed to them. This was essentially the prophetic point of view and it was in this connection that the law codes were presented in a historical setting. Thus we see that the prophetic literature of the Old Testament included the historical narratives as well as the writings attributed to the prophets for whom books were named.

THE PENTATEUCH
Summary

The first five books of the Old Testament were, according to both Jewish and Christian traditions, attributed to Moses until comparatively recent times. To be sure there were some exceptions, but in general we may say that it was not until the era of the movement known as "Higher Criticism" that the Mosaic authorship of these books was brought into question. Now there is almost universal agreement among Biblical scholars that the Pentateuch is composed of at least four separate and distinct narratives written by different persons who were widely separated in point of time. Indeed, it seems highly probable that within each of these four documents it is possible to recognize the work of more than one author. The evidence in support of this view is overwhelming. Nothing in the first four of these books asserts, or even suggests, that Moses was the author. Deuteronomy is presented as though it were an address delivered by Moses, but the contents of the book indicate quite clearly that it was written a long time after the death of Moses. It was a fairly common practice among Hebrew authors to write as though the words they used had been spoken a long time before.

The earliest of these four main narratives is known as the *Early Judean History*. Because the author is unknown he is designated by the letter *J*, since it is believed that he was a prophet of the southern, or Judean, kingdom. The narrative begins with the story of creation as it is recorded in the second chapter of the book of Genesis. It concludes with an account of the establishment of the monarchy in the land of Canaan. There are several distinctive characteristics of this history. Yahweh is the name used for the deity. It stands for a god who is conceived in terms that are crudely anthropomorphic. He possesses a physical body, walks in the Garden of Eden during the cool or the day, talks directly with Adam, and is a dinner guest in the tent of Abraham. He behaves in a manner which resembles in many respects the typical chief of a primitive tribe. The place names which are used are ones which belong to the southern kingdom. The ethical standards which are implied are on a somewhat lower plane than those of later narratives. The various parts of the history are organized in a manner which sets forth the author's conception of the divine purpose to be realized on earth and the reasons why its fulfillment has been delayed.

This history appears to have been written about 850 B.C. The source materials used for its composition included not only the written documents available at that time but a number of traditions which had been passed on orally from older generations. In the creation story man is formed out of the dust of the earth, and Eve, the first woman, is created from Adam's rib. The story of the fall, which has to do with the eating of forbidden fruit, is followed by an account of the two sons Cain and Abel. Because sin had become so widespread over the face of the earth, Yahweh caused the great flood to appear but spared Noah and all that was with him in the ark.

After the flood Noah pronounces a curse on Canaan and gives blessings to Shem and Japheth. Abraham's call is followed by an account of his journey to Egypt. After his return a promise is made to him concerning the birth of a son and the inheritance of the land of Canaan by his descendants. Although Abraham and his wife have reached an advanced age, Isaac is born in fulfillment of the promise. Isaac's two sons Jacob and Esau are said to have struggled in the mother's womb before they were born, thus indicating the strife that was to continue for centuries between the Israelites and the Edomites. Jacob deceives his father and tricks his brother Esau out of the birthright. He then goes to a distant land where he marries the two daughters of Laban and enters into an agreement whereby he obtains a large share of his uncle's property. On his return home with the members of his family, he meets his brother and the two are reconciled.

Jacob's favorite son, Joseph, is sold by his brothers into slavery but eventually he comes to hold a powerful place in the government of Egypt. Jacob with his sons and their families move to Egypt because of the famine in the land of Canaan. Their descendants increased in number and this caused an Egyptian Pharaoh to become alarmed lest the Israelite colony become too powerful. Accordingly, he began a policy of oppression which placed on the Hebrews burdens that were greater than they could bear. Moses was summoned by Yahweh to deliver his people from this oppression. After a series of plagues had been visited upon the Egyptians, the Hebrews left the land where they had become enslaved and began their march through the wilderness toward the land of Canaan. After a description of difficulties which they encountered during this march, the author concludes his history with an account of their entrance into the land and the conquering of a portion of it.

The second of the four narratives is known as the *Ephraimite History*. The author is designated by the letter *E* for two reasons. It is the first letter in the word Ephraimite, which is used interchangeably with the northern kingdom. Since the place names which occur in this history belong to the northern kingdom, it is assumed that the author was a native of this place. The second reason is that E is the first letter in the word *Elohim*, which is the name for the deity in that part of the history which precedes the story of Moses and the burning bush. In our present Bibles the J and E histories have been interwoven so as to present a single narrative. However, a careful analysis can reveal with a fair degree of accuracy the materials which belonged to each of the original histories. There are several distinctive characteristics of the E narrative, such as the use of the term Elohim, place names belonging to the north, a more advanced conception of the deity, higher ethical standards implied in the stories concerning the patriarchs, strong opposition to idol worship, and an unfavorable attitude toward the establishment of a monarchy with a king to rule over the people.

This history is believed to have been written about 750 B.C., which is a century later than the J narrative. Although these two histories are in many respects parallel versions of the same events, E begins with the story of Abraham and makes no references to what may have happened prior to that time. The stories pertaining to the patriarchs Abraham, Isaac, Jacob, and Joseph are told in a more favorable light than in the J history. This indicates something of an advance in ethical ideals, for these heroes of the

Israelite people are not regarded as guilty of the acts of deception which were condoned in J's account of the same events. The story of the sacrifice of Isaac occurs only in the E narrative. Here the purpose of the story is twofold. The author wants to illustrate perfect obedience to the will of God on the part of Abraham and he also wants to make it clear that human sacrifices are no longer required by the deity. Animals may be substituted in their place.

The great masterpiece of E's narrative is the Joseph story, which is related in greater detail than J had reported. The underlying motive of the story is that a divine purpose is being realized through the course of human events, even though the individuals who are involved in it at the time may be entirely unconscious of it. It was Moses who, according to E, introduced the name of Yahweh to the Hebrew people. Although Yahweh may be regarded as the same god who appeared to the early patriarchs, he was not known by this name until the time of Moses. It was not until Moses returned from a lengthy sojourn in the land of Midian that Yahweh appeared to him in a burning bush and called upon him to deliver his own people from the oppression of the Egyptian Pharaoh. When Moses protested that he was slow of speech and unable to present his demands before the Egyptian ruler, it was arranged that his brother Aaron should be a prophet or spokesman for him.

The experiences during the march through the wilderness are described at considerable length. When the people are encamped near Mount Sinai, Moses goes up into the mount and receives from Yahweh the tables of the law. The story of Aaron and the golden calves is told in a manner that is intended to make idol worship appear ridiculous. Moses was not permitted to enter into the land of Canaan. Joshua was chosen to be the leader in his place. After achieving remarkable success in the matter of getting established in the new country, he gives a formal farewell address. An account is given of an important meeting at Schechem where representatives of the different tribes met and formed themselves into a confederacy. This action introduced the period of the judges, which was designed as a form of government in which Yahweh would rule by communicating his will directly to those who had been appointed to receive it. This type of organization continued until the people clamored for a king to rule over them.

The third narrative, designated by the letter *D*, is the one found in our present book of Deuteronomy. Like the other narratives it appears to be the work of several authors. Its distinctive characteristic is the body of laws which forms the main core of the book. These laws are recorded in chapters 12-28. Chapters 5-11 consist of a hortatory introduction to the laws. The remaining chapters are believed to be later additions to the original book. These were added in order that the entire book might be regarded as an integral part of a complete history which reaches from the time of creation to the post-exilic period.

Although the introductory statements indicate that the words included in this part of the history were spoken by Moses, the contents of the book tell a different story. Many, if not most, of the specific laws which are set forth are not appropriate to the times of Moses. Indeed, they are designed to deal with situations which did not arise until long after the era of Moses. The story of the finding of a law book in the Temple which is recorded in II Kings 22 is believed to be a reference to the Deuteronomic code of laws. If this is correct the laws were formulated by disciples of the eighth-century prophets and were designed to correct those conditions concerning which Amos, Hosea, and Isaiah had protested so vigorously. Especially prominent in this code is the law of the Central Sanctuary, which forbade the offering of sacrifices at any other place than the particular one designated for that purpose. Obviously, it was the Temple in Jerusalem that the authors had in mind but the naming of that place would have been inappropriate in a document attributed to Moses. Actually we know it was not until the book had been discovered in the Temple during the reign of Josiah that his particular law had been either recognized or enforced.

Another important law was known as the Year of Release. It provided that at the end of each six-year period all the property that had been forfeited to satisfy debts should be returned to its original owners. This was intended not only to prevent an undue accumulation of wealth on the part of a few but also to provide new opportunities for those who had been deprived of their possessions through unfortunate circumstances over which they had no control. Other laws were for the purpose of protecting those who had been falsely accused. By fleeing to one of the cities of refuge the accused person would be safe until the charge had been thoroughly investigated.

Not all of the laws of Deuteronomy were of an ethical nature. Ritualistic requirements, such as the prohibition of eating certain kinds of meat, sowing mixed seed in the same field, purification rites, and numerous ceremonies, were included along with the other laws. The nationalistic character of this legislation is illustrated in the fact that Hebrews and non-Hebrews were not subject to the same requirements. For instance, animals that had died a natural death could not be sold to the Hebrews for food but they could be sold to foreigners. The treatment of slaves was another instance in which Israelites were entitled to privileges denied to foreigners.

The hortatory introduction to the law codes is presented as an address given by Moses. The motive which should prompt obedience to these laws is gratitude for the way in which Yahweh had delivered his people from bondage in Egypt. The Sabbath, for example, should be observed as a memorial of their deliverance and it should constantly remind them of their obligation to treat with kindness the laborers in their employ. Later additions supplement the earlier portions of Deuteronomy by putting all of it under the same historical setting. Blessings are pronounced upon those who obey all the statutes and ordinances of the book and a curse is pronounced on all those who refuse to obey.

The fourth and last of these Pentateuchal narratives is called the *Late Priestly History* and it is designated by the letter *P*. The date for its composition is usually placed somewhere near 450 B.C. It is called a priestly history because it represents the point of view generally held by the priests, who were inclined to place the greater emphasis upon ritualistic requirements. Although written in the form of a history, it contains a number of law codes. One of these is known as the *Holiness Code;* it is recorded in Leviticus 17-26. The P narrative includes many other regulations pertaining chiefly to the place, manner, and forms of worship. It was one of the chief duties of the priests during the post-exilic period to see that these regulations were enforced.

The history begins with the creation story as it is reported in the first chapter of the book of Genesis. Although this narrative is now interwoven with the J and E histories, its unique characteristics make it somewhat easier to distinguish the materials which belong to it. For one thing it has a formal and legalistic style of writing. There is a concern for exact and precise statements. For example, in the creation story it was not sufficient to state that the heavens and the earth were created by divine act. It was necessary to state exactly what had been accomplished on each of the six days of the creation week. The age of each of the early patriarchs was recorded in an exact number of years. The dates when Noah entered into the ark and again when he left it are also recorded. It is evident, too, that the author's interpretation of history had much to do with the recording of particular events. Because it was believed that the average life span was proportionate to the amount of sin which had been committed, the life of the earliest inhabitants was said to have been much longer than it was at the time when the history was written. In fact, they report that people lived to be eight or nine hundred years old. But this was before sin had become so prevalent in the world. As sin increased, the life span became shorter and shorter.

Because it was important in the post-exilic period to give a new emphasis to the religious institutions which had been neglected, an attempt was made to show the very ancient origin of each of them. Thus we find the story of creation culminating in the institution of the Sabbath. The Deuteronomic narrative had indicated that the Sabbath was to be observed as a memorial of the deliverance from Egypt, but in the P narrative it is more ancient than that. It goes back to the time of Adam and the creation of the world. The story of Noah and the flood provides a setting for the laws which prohibit murder and the eating of blood. Circumcision, which had come to have a deep religious significance for the Hebrews, is now said to have been introduced by Abraham, and the feast of the Passover was established by Moses. In this way each of these four institutions was shown to be not only of ancient origin but introduced by one of the great characters of the past.

The history of the periods covered in the J and E narratives is passed over quickly, except for those particular points that needed special emphasis. The story of the march through the wilderness included a great deal of material not found in the older narratives. This new material had to do very largely with detailed instruction concerning the offering of sacrifices and other ritualistic performances. The reason for this was the obvious desire on the part of the authors to show that the priestly requirements of the post-exilic age were really in force from the time when the Hebrews left Egypt. Although the law of the Central Sanctuary, which had to do with the Temple in Jerusalem, was actually a later development, the P historians explain the ancient character of the law by their account of a moving sanctuary made according to instruction given to Moses and carried about with them as the Hebrews journeyed through the wilderness. It was no more than a tent but it contained rooms and equipment that corresponded to the Temple of later years. Of the many ceremonies which are described in detail, the most important are those pertaining to the services to be performed on the day of Atonement.

Commentary

The Pentateuch, or what came to be known as the Torah or book of the Law, was regarded as the most authoritative and most highly inspired of all the Old Testament writings. There were several reasons for this. One of them was the fact that these books contain the laws given to the Israelites by Yahweh. These laws, like the source from which they were derived, were eternal and would forever remain the standard by which the conduct of the people would be judged. Because Moses had long been recognized as the great lawgiver who transmitted the words of Yahweh to the people of Israel, it seemed appropriate to attribute the writing of all the books of the law to him. Actually we know from the contents of the Old

Testament itself that the concept of divine law and its application to the problems and situations that occurred in Hebrew history was a developmental process which took place over long periods of time. Attributing all of these laws to Moses was in no sense an intention to deceive the people but rather a device for indicating the eternal character of the laws and a continuation of the spirit and purpose of the work of Moses. Then, too, the laws constituted the basis upon which the covenant relationship between Yahweh and the Hebrew people had been established. The significance of the covenant idea in the Old Testament can scarcely be overestimated. The prophets were constantly making reference to it by insisting that the fate of Israel would always be determined by the extent to which the people were faithful or unfaithful to the obligations placed upon them by the covenant.

JOSHUA, JUDGES, AND SAMUEL

Summary

The book of Joshua consists of twenty-four chapters. Approximately the first half of the book is an extension of the history recorded in Deuteronomy. The remainder appears to have been added by authors of the late priestly history. The story of the conquest of Canaan is told briefly and in a manner which indicates that it was accomplished easily and within a relatively short period of time. The crossing of the Jordan River was attended by Yahweh's miraculous intervention reminiscent of the crossing of the Red Sea which followed the exodus from Egypt. In commemoration of the event twelve stones were taken from the bed of the river and set up as a monument. The first city to be attacked was Jericho, where the walls came tumbling down at the moment when the trumpet blasts were heard. Achan's stealing of a wedge of gold, together with a fine Babylonian garment, is given as the reason why the Hebrews failed at first to capture the city of Ai. Not until punishment had been meted out for this sin did the city fall into their hands.

In accordance with the instruction which he had received, Joshua gathered in one place representatives of all the people and delivered to them the statutes and ordinances which had been given by Moses. In a battle with the Gibeonites Joshua commanded the sun and moon to stand still, with the result that the day was lengthened, thus enabling his forces to achieve a remarkable victory over their enemies. The latter chapters of the book describe the division of the land among the various tribes. The authors of this book were evidently interested in personalities. They had a very high regard for Joshua, ranking him as second only to Moses. The farewell address which this hero delivered before all Israel praised Yahweh for the victories he had given them and counseled the people to remain faithful to the god who had already done so much in their behalf.

The book of Judges is really a continuation of the history in Joshua. Its central theme is the settlement in the land of Canaan. This was the period which preceded the establishment of the monarchy. The leaders of the people were known as judges. However, their chief function was not that of deciding cases of law but rather that of providing political and military leadership in times of crises. These crises occurred one after another in rapid succession, indicating quite clearly that after the death of Joshua the situation which the Israelites faced was one of chaos. Whenever conditions became intolerable a leader would arise and deliver his people from the hands of the enemy. But the victory would never bring about anything more than temporary relief. Within a short time a new crisis would develop and the cycle of events would be repeated.

The first judge, or deliverer, was Othniel. He brought victory to the Israelites after they had suffered eight years of oppression by the king of Mesopotamia. Then came Ehud, who delivered them from the Moabites. Deborah, who was both a judge and a prophetess, sent out a call to the various tribes to unite in a battle against the Canaanites. Responding to her call, the Israelites defeated the armies of Sisera at the battle of Megiddo. Gideon was another judge who delivered the people of Israel. This time it was the Midianites who caused the trouble. The story of Gideon is related at considerable length, for he was regarded as one of the better judges. As a result of his activities the land is said to have had rest for a period of forty years. Jephthah was the judge who made a vow to Yahweh that if he would grant him victory in his war with the Ammonites he would offer as a sacrifice whatever would first come out of his house on his return. The victory was achieved and on his way home he was met first of all by his own daughter. With great emotion he told her of his vow and shortly thereafter he carried it out.

Samson was one of the more prominent judges who tricked the Philistines on several occasions. At one time he slew thousands of them with the jawbone of an ass. His affair with Delilah, who betrayed him to the Philistines, cost him his eyesight, but in the end he was restored to Yahweh's favor and he was able to pull down the temple which housed the Philistine god Dagon. Many other judges are mentioned and concerning a few of them some interesting stories are related. The historian of this period was convinced that Israel should have had a different type of leadership. His attitude is expressed in these words: "In those days there was no king in Israel, and each man did what was right in his own eyes."

The two books of Samuel record an important transition in political organization. The period of the judges came to an end with Samuel, who is also referred to as a seer and a prophet. He was the one who anointed Saul to be the first king of Israel. The history of the monarchy which is contained in these books is believed to have been compiled during the reign of Josiah, who was king of Judah. Because of the reformation which he inaugurated Josiah was regarded as a great king. It was believed that under his leadership the hopes and aspirations for the future of Israel would soon be realized. But if kingship meant so much at this time, it seemed reasonable enough to suppose that Israel's troubles during the early period of the settlement in Canaan were due to the fact that they had no king to rule over them. This is the idea which is conveyed in certain parts of the book of Samuel. But since the compiler of the history used source materials of which some expressed an opposite idea, the story as we have it now is a bit confusing. On the one hand we are told that the establishment of the monarchy was a great achievement, and on the other that it was Israel's greatest mistake. According to the latter view, Samuel had warned the people of the dangers that were involved in having a king, and it was only after their persistent demands that Yahweh relented and allowed them to have their own way.

Because the career of Samuel marks an important transition point in the history of the Hebrew people, many stories concerning him were preserved. We read that he was dedicated to Yahweh even before he was born. His birth was a miraculous event, since prior to this time his mother Hannah had been childless. While only a small boy he was taken to the home of Eli the priest so that he might be reared under influences that would prepare him for his future work. Yahweh called to him in the night and spoke a message of reproof which he was to deliver to Eli. When the elders of Israel had gathered for a consultation concerning their political future they called upon Samuel to select someone to be anointed as king. Here we have two conflicting accounts. According to one of them he protests vigorously against a movement of this kind. In the other account Saul arrives at Samuel's house after a prolonged search for his father's lost asses. Samuel has been warned in advance of his coming and knowing that Yahweh's chosen is before him he makes arrangements for him to be anointed as king.

The brief account of Saul's reign appears also to have been based on conflicting source materials. The most probable explanation is that the sources used were written by friends and by foes of the idea of a monarchy for Israel. Saul's disobedience in sparing the life of the Amalekite king along with animals which were offered as a sacrifice was bitterly denounced by Samuel. This failure on the part of Saul is used as an introduction to the story of David. In response to instruction which he received from Yahweh, Samuel went to the home of a certain Jesse who had several sons, one of whom was to be selected to become king in place of Saul. Although David was the youngest of the sons, he was the one who was chosen. Eventually Saul became jealous of David and his antagonism is illustrated in a number of different stories. I Samuel closes with an account of the war with the Philistines and Saul's tragic death on Mt. Gilboa.

II Samuel is concerned almost entirely with the career of David. An excerpt from the book of Yashur reports a eulogy spoken by David in commemoration of Saul and Jonathan. An account is given of the way in which David was made king first over Judah and later over all of Israel. The story of Abner's death is followed by a short poem in which David expresses lamentation over the way in which Saul's trusted general had met his death. We are told how David captured the city of Jerusalem and made it the headquarters of his kingdom. The ark is brought to Jerusalem and we are informed concerning many of David's victories. His sin against Uriah is reported and also the way in which he was reproved by Nathan the prophet. Absalom's rebellion is reported at considerable length and the book ends with the story of David's sin in numbering the people of Israel.

Commentary

The history that is recorded in these books represents the point of view of post-exilic writers. In their account of the events which followed the entrance of the Hebrews into the land of Canaan, they were influenced by the religious ideals and practices that were current at the time when they lived. The purpose of the history was not primarily that of preserving an accurate record of what had happened in the past but rather that of emphasizing the religious lessons that had been illustrated in the course of events. The Deuteronomic law of the Central Sanctuary as well as the regulations embodied in the Holiness Code and the detailed instructions of the Priests' Code were considered extremely important for the preservation of the Hebrew religion. By projecting these ideals and institutions back to the early history of their people, it could be shown that they were not innovations invented by contemporary priests but instead they were continuations of principles that had been recognized as far back as the time of Moses. Further support for these institutions would be provided by showing that the course of Hebrew history had been determined primarily by the attitude of these people with regard to the requirements specified in these codes.

In the writing of this history the authors made use of older source materials, including such documents as the "Book of the Wars of Yahweh," the "Book of Yashur the Upright," the "Song of Deborah," and other fragments of the early literature which were available to them. The primitive character of some of these sources can be understood from the fact that they were produced in an early age going back as far as the period of the united kingdom and in some instances even earlier than that. This explains in part the strange and barbaric stories which have been incorporated into the history. Actions which would not have been condoned at all in later times are related without any apparent censure or blame. These tales in their original form represent a period of Hebrew history which preceded the teaching of the great prophets and the corresponding development of ethical ideals.

Because the sources used were produced by men who held opposite views toward such institutions as the establishment of the monarchy, we can see why it is that conflicting accounts of the same event can be found side by side in the history. In some instances the two different accounts are presented without any attempt to reconcile the disagreements. At other times it is possible to detect explanatory passages which have been inserted by editors and copyists in an attempt to harmonize the accounts with one another. In spite of these conflicts, one notes that throughout this history there is the underlying conception of a moral order that characterizes the historical process. This illustrates what the Hebrew writers believed to be the divine element in history. Obedience to the commands of Yahweh was certain to bring about consequences quite different from the ones that were sure to follow disobedience of these commands. To the prophetic historians this meant in the long run the choice between life and death.

KINGS, CHRONICLES, EZRA, AND NEHEMIAH

Summary

In the two books of Kings we have what has often been called the *Deuteronomic History of the Kings of Israel and Judah*. It has been given this name because of the prominence attached to the Deuteronomic law of the Central Sanctuary. The author considers the attitude of Israel's kings toward the observance of this law as the most important factor in their various reigns. It was their conduct in this respect which determined more than anything else whether they did that which was evil or that which was good in the sight of Yahweh. Although some of the kings ruled for a comparatively long time and others occupied the throne for only a brief period, all were judged by the same standard. Any king who failed to destroy the high places or permitted the people to offer sacrifices at any place other than the Temple in Jerusalem was said to have done evil in the sight of Yahweh and in this way he was responsible for the disasters which fell upon the nation.

The history in Kings takes up the story of the kingdom at the point where it ended in the books of Samuel and continues the account until the time of Josiah, king of Judah. The work is divided into three parts, dealing with the united kingdom under David and Solomon, the parallel history of the divided kingdom until the fall of Samaria, and finally with the southern kingdom, or Judah, alone. The author used a number of sources such as the "Book of the Acts of Solomon," the "Temple Annals," the "Elisha Stories," and other documents which reported on particular events. He obviously took from these sources only the materials that were suited to his purpose. In this way he could shape the materials in a way that would bring out the lessons he wanted to teach.

He begins with an account of how Solomon was chosen to be the successor of King David. The author of this history was evidently an admirer of Solomon, for he credited him with great wisdom in administering the affairs of the kingdom. He tells of the prayer which he offered at the dedication of the Temple and of his wise decisions in dealing with difficult problems. He does mention the fact that Solomon did not destroy the high places of worship and that he brought many foreign wives to the court in Jerusalem. Although some excuse is provided for this conduct, the author suggests quite strongly that herein lies the main reason for the rebellion and division of the monarchy which occurred after Solomon's death.

The second part of the history follows a very definite pattern in describing the activities of each of the kings in both the northern and the southern kingdoms. The narrator begins by telling when it was that the king began to reign and how long he continued to do so. He next states whether he was a good or an evil king. In some instances the record of events which took place during the reign of a particular king is fairly long, while in others it is comparatively short. But always the standard of judgment is the same. It is the attitude of the king toward the law of the Central Sanctuary. To permit the worship to be carried on at any of the local shrines, or so-called high places, is regarded as a more serious offense than any of the forms of social injustice. Since the only legitimate sanctuary was located in Jerusalem, which was now the capital of the southern kingdom, the kings of the north did not have access to it and consequently if they were to authorize the conduct of any worship at all it would have to be at some local place. This seems to be the chief reason why the author opens his account of each one of the kings of the north by saying, "He did that which was evil in the sight of Yahweh." Of course the kings of the south did not always destroy the high places either, but he was more charitable in dealing with them. He usually found some excuse for their failure in this respect. An interesting feature in this part of the history is the system of chronology that is used. The dates pertaining to each are recorded in terms of the number of years the corresponding ruler of the other kingdom had reigned. For example, a northern king is said to have begun his reign during the fifth year of the corresponding king of the southern kingdom.

The third part of the history covers the period of Judah alone. The northern kingdom has gone into captivity because of the transgressions of the inhabitants, and now it is through the southern kingdom alone that the hopes of the Hebrew people are to be realized. The reign of King Hezekiah is described at greater length than those of most of the other kings because the author regarded him as a great reformer. The invasion of the Judean kingdom by Sennacherib, the Assyrian ruler, is reported and also the visit to Jerusalem of Merodach-baladin of Babylon. The reign which lasted for over fifty years is passed over lightly and the same is true of that of his son and successor Amon, who was assassinated. With the coming to the throne of King Josiah the author expresses great optimism, for it was during his reign that the law book was discovered in the Temple and the great reformation inaugurated. It was probably at this point that the author ended his history for it is assumed that Josiah was still king when he wrote. Later writers extended the Deuteronomic history but it is in the books of Judges, Samuel, and other portions of the Old Testament that their work is recorded.

If the Deuteronomic law may be said to have been the standard of judgment in the books of Kings, it is the Priests Code that is the standard in the book of Chronicles. This history appears to have been written somewhat later than the one in Kings. The date that is usually given is somewhere around 300 B.C. The authors have the advantage of using as source materials the Deuteronomic history as well as the many other documents which had appeared prior to this date. Apparently they accepted the idea set forth in the older histories that personal suffering as well as national disasters were punishments for wrongdoing, while long life and material prosperity were a reward for righteous conduct.

This conception of history was adequate to explain some things that had happened but there were other events that seemed to contradict this view. For instance, King Uzziah, whose reign preceded Isaiah's call to the prophetic office, was regarded as one of the ablest and best kings of Judah and yet he was smitten with leprosy and died in a leper colony. Then too there was king Manasseh who, judged by all the accepted standards of both priests and prophets, was a wicked man but he reigned for more than half a century and died a natural death. Josiah, the good king who started the Deuteronomic reformation and followed as closely as he could the teachings of the great prophets, was slain on the field of battle and his son was taken to Egypt as a prisoner. The chronicler felt that it was necessary to provide an explanation for these events and he did so. Believing as he did that Yahweh has something to do with the course of events he interpreted the entire course of Hebrew history from the point of view of the laws and regulations that were embodied in the Priests Code.

The introduction to this history consisted of a brief sketch of the period from Adam to David. The career of David the chronicler idealized quite in contrast with the record preserved in the books of Samuel. The law of the Central Sanctuary was projected back into the early period by identifying it with the tabernacle which the Israelites carried with them in their march through the wilderness. The Priests Code, too, is presumed to have been in force during the early periods of Hebrew history. No mention is made of the kings of northern Israel, since it was assumed that the people in that kingdom were no better than the heathen and in consequence of their behavior they were no longer to be counted among the true people of Israel.

The books of Ezra and Nehemiah were also a part of the history produced by the authors of Chronicles. Here the story which had been reported up to the time of the Babylonian exile was now continued into the post-exilic period. The book of Ezra contains ten chapters, six of which are concerned almost entirely with a recounting of the events which led to the return of the Jews to Jerusalem. Ezra is the one who had in his possession a royal decree authorizing him to make the return along with all the Jews who wished to return with him. They were permitted to bring with them all the contributions that had been made toward the project. As soon as they returned they built an altar and later they rebuilt the Temple, having overcome the opposition that had been raised by the Samaritans. Ezra protests against the intermarriage of Jews with foreigners and insists that the guilty persons shall obtain divorces from their spouses.

The book of Nehemiah consists of three parts. In the first one Nehemiah is presented as the cupbearer to Artaxerxes, the Persian king who granted him permission to visit the city of Jerusalem. During this visit he takes an active part in helping to rebuild the walls that had been demolished. In the second part it is Ezra rather than Nehemiah who is the center of attention. Ezra gathers the people into one great assembly and reads to them from the book of the Law. The third part contains a number of miscellaneous items, including lists of those who returned from the exile. The book closes with an account of Nehemiah's second visit to Jerusalem after an interval of twelve years.

Commentary

With the books of Ezra and Nehemiah the historical survey from Adam to the rebuilding of the Temple in the post-exilic period was approximately completed. The final result included the word of many different authors who lived at different times and who represented in some instances opposite points of view. The work as a whole began with the Judean and the Ephraimite histories, which form a part of the Pentateuch, and it was continued at various intervals by Deuteronomic and Priestly historians. These later writers not only used as source materials the older narratives which were available to them but they supplemented and revised the accounts in the light of the ideals and institutions that were dominant when they did their work. The rewriting of the J and E histories did not, however, replace the earlier accounts, for their value and prestige had been too well established for them to be put aside. Hence, the newer histories have been preserved in the Old Testament along with the older ones.

The book of Kings tells the story as it was seen by an enthusiastic supporter of the Deuteronomic code of laws. While this code does include both moral and ritualistic requirements, the later historian places the major emphasis on the ones having to do with the ritual. Perhaps one of the reasons for this is the fact that outward observances can be enforced in a manner which is not possible in the case of moral requirements, which involve the motive as well as the overt act. The work of supplementing and revising the older histories continued over a long period of time and with an increasing emphasis on the many details having to do with the place, form, time, and manner of worship. This is what one would expect of the Priestly historians. This does not mean that they ignored moral matters. They wanted, no less than the prophets, to bring the people into harmony with the will of Yahweh. But it was the business of the priests to conduct the various forms of worship and it seemed obvious to them that obedience to divine commands was a prerequisite to any satisfactory relations with Yahweh. It is this point of view that is expressed so clearly in the books of Chronicles and Ezra and Nehemiah.

THE WISDOM LITERATURE

In the book of Jeremiah reference is made to three distinct groups of people known as the priests, the prophets, and the sages, or wise men. Of these three the prophets were responsible for the largest portion of Old Testament writings. They produced not only the books which bear the names of particular prophets but the historical writings which include a record of the specific laws and requirements which pertained to the work of the priests. There are, however, three books in the Old Testament that represent the work of Israel's teachers, or so-called wise men. They are the books of Job, Ecclesiastes, and Proverbs. In contrast with the prophetic writings, they did not preface their remarks with a "thus saith Yahweh," but instead they appealed to reason and common sense in support of what they had to say. Their writings are characterized by a broad and universal appeal which avoids the nationalistic spirit so prevalent in many of the prophetic writings. Because the sages addressed themselves to the problems that arise in everyday living, their counsel and advice was applicable to non-Jews just as much as it was to the people of Israel. They spoke to individuals rather than to the nation and they considered problems which had nothing to do with race or nationality. If the religion of the Old Testament can be said to have reached its greatest heights in the teachings of the prophets, it can also be said that in the work of the sages it reached its greatest breadth.

THE BOOK OF JOB
Summary

The book of Job is often referred to as one of the great classics in the literature of the world. Its subject matter is the all-important question which has to do with the suffering of innocent persons. Why, in a world over which Yahweh has jurisdiction, should innocent persons have to suffer when at the same time the wicked escape suffering and are permitted to have comfort and security? Although the experiences of the Jewish people had caused them to wonder about it a great deal, there is nothing about this problem that is peculiar to any one nation or group of people. It is a universal problem and one that sooner or later is encountered by all persons. Some of the Hebrew prophets had attempted to deal with this question insofar as it affected the nation as a whole, but it is in the book of Job that the author deals with it on an individual basis. The book in its present form falls into five parts which may be designated as the prologue, the symposium, the speeches of Elihu, the nature poems, and the epilogue. The book as a whole appears to have been written as a direct challenge to the time-honored doctrine that in this life people are rewarded or punished according to their merits.

The prologue, which consists of the first two chapters of the book, is believed to have been based on an older folktale in which a wager is made between Yahweh and Satan. Satan has charged that no one serves Yahweh except for selfish reasons. Yahweh does not admit this and in support of his opinion he presents Job, who is a righteous man, "one who fears God and eschews evil." In order to prove to Satan that Job's loyalty is not for the sake of a material reward, Yahweh permits Satan to take away from Job all of the material benefits he has received and even to afflict him with the most severe and excruciating pain. Through all of this suffering Job does not murmur or complain. His response to it all is, "The Lord hath given, and the Lord hath taken away, blessed be the name of the Lord." Job's wife urges him to "curse God and die" in order to gain relief from his suffering. Three friends come from afar and express their sympathy by remaining silent and by clothing themselves in sackcloth and sitting in ashes. In all of this it is said that Job sinned not; neither did he complain.

The symposium tells a very different story. It consists of speeches by Job and by each of the three friends—Eliphaz the Temanite, Bildad the Shuhite, and Zophar the Naamathite. In the first speech Job curses the day that he was born, insisting that life under the conditions which he must bear is not worthwhile. He sees no justice at all in the way he must suffer, since he is conscious of no wrongdoing. To this speech Eliphaz replies that righteous people do not suffer. It is only the wicked who are tormented in this fashion. For Job to declare himself innocent is to charge Yahweh with injustice and it is not reasonable that a man should be more just than God. He argues that in God's sight no human beings are righteous. All have sinned and any suffering which they must endure is only a just punishment for their transgressions. Bildad adds his support to what Eliphaz has said by insisting that God does not pervert justice; neither does he ever act unrighteously. Zophar goes even further in his accusations against Job. He says Job is not being punished as much as he deserves, for it must be remembered that Yahweh is not only a just but a merciful God and mercy always means treating one better than he deserves.

To each of these speeches Job makes an effective reply. He challenges his accusers to point out any evil deed that he has committed. If he has failed simply because he is a mortal being, it is not his fault for he was created that way. His conduct has been as good as that of his accusers. After the first round of speeches the cycle is repeated, with Job again making a reply after each one has spoken. In the third cycle of speeches only Eliphaz and Bildad speak again. In Job's final reply he makes a masterful defense of his own position, at the conclusion of which we are told that "the words of Job are ended."

The speeches of Elihu represent a further attempt to find justification for Job's affliction. Elihu admits that the arguments of the three friends have been adequately refuted by Job, but he believes he can present other ones that will show how Job has been in the wrong. He suggests that Job's suffering may be a warning so that he won't sin. He then falls back into a repetition of the same arguments the friends had used.

The nature poems are presented as speeches of Yahweh which are addressed to Job. They picture in the most exquisite language the wonders and the grandeur of the created universe. It is doubtful if one could find more beautiful or inspiring poetry in the language of any people. But beautiful as they are, they do not deal with Job's problem at all. It is true they contrast the power and wisdom of the deity with the inferior lot of human beings, but they still leave unanswered the question of why it is that innocent people have to suffer in the manner which Job has experienced. In the epilogue which is found in the last chapter of the book, we are told that Job acknowledged the justice of Yahweh and repented of all that he had said in his own defense. After this Yahweh recompensed Job by returning to him all the material wealth that had been taken away from him and even doubling the amount of property which he possessed.

Commentary

The book of Job does not present any concrete solution to the problem of the suffering of innocent persons. So far as the symposium is concerned, the purpose of the author seems to have been none other than to challenge the view presented by both prophets and historians to the effect that suffering is in itself evidence of wrongdoing. For centuries it had been accepted as true that, since Yahweh is a just ruler of the universe, the distribution of rewards and punishments must be in strict accordance with what people actually deserve. The author of the symposium was convinced that this is not true. In order to make his position clear he constructed the story of a righteous man named Job. As an introduction to his theme he made use of a popular folktale in which a good man suffers in order to prove to Satan that he does not serve Yahweh for selfish reasons. That the author of the symposium did not accept this solution to the problem is shown very clearly in the arguments between Job and the three friends. Job's final speech in his own defense was probably where the original book ended.

The skeptical character of the symposium with its challenge to time-honored views would probably have kept the book of Job out of the canon of Old Testament writings had not some additions been made to the original book. The speeches of Elihu appear to have been added for the purpose of giving to the book an interpretation more in accord with the older views of the prophets. It is quite possible that the same is true of the nature poems which are presented as words spoken by Yahweh. While it is true that neither the speeches of Elihu nor the nature poems give any direct answer to the question of why innocent persons have to suffer, their presence in the book as a whole does at least suggest there may be a reason for it which human beings are unable to grasp. The epilogue is, of course, a kind of anticlimax, inasmuch as it does tend to support the charges made by Satan in the prologue. It does, however, present an ending to the book quite in keeping with the older or more orthodox position.

ECCLESIASTES

Summary

The book of Ecclesiastes is an essay on the topic "Is life worthwhile?." It is a strange book, for the author answers this question in the negative. He considers the various ends or goals for which people live and he finds that each of them brings only "vanity and vexation of spirit." One translation reads, "all is vanity and a chasing after wind." He refers to himself as an elderly person, a man of considerable means, and one who has tried about all of the ways that people pursue in their quest for a meaningful life. He has gone in for pleasure and found that in the end it is self-defeating. He has tried riches and found that they do not satisfy. He has sought fame and found that it too is an empty thing. He has even tried the pursuit of wisdom and found that it likewise fails to satisfy the human spirit. The more one learns the more dissatisfied he becomes with that which he has already attained.

There are those who have followed the course of justice, believing that they will be rewarded for so doing. The author of Ecclesiastes is convinced that this is not true. His observation tells him that the righteous man fares no better than the wicked man. There are times when he doesn't fare even as well. Regardless of how a man lives, when he dies he will be forgotten and the fact is that death comes to the righteous and the wicked alike. The author appears to be familiar with the belief on the part of some people that rewards and punishments will be meted out to individuals in a future life that is beyond the grave, but he takes no stock in this notion. He tells us that the death of a man is comparable to that of a beast. He asks ironically, "Who knows whether the spirit of man goes upward and the spirit of the beast goes down to the earth?" He says emphatically, "They all have the same breath, and man has no advantage over the beasts; for all is vanity." He does not believe in progress but is committed to a cycle theory of history. "What has been is what will be, and what has been done is what will be done; and there is nothing new under the sun." It is true that each generation thinks it has developed something new, but this is because the achievements of former generations have been forgotten just as those of the present generation will not be remembered in the future. Furthermore, he sees no point in trying to make the world better. "What is crooked cannot be made straight, and what is lacking cannot be numbered." The desires of men can never be satisfied, for the more one sees the more he wants to see, and the more things he acquires the less satisfied he becomes with what he has obtained.

The author is indeed a cynic but at the same time he is a gentle cynic who has not become embittered toward the world. He realizes this is the way things are and he is resolved to make the best of them. Unlike the author of Job, who is all wrought up over the fact that innocent people have to suffer, this writer accepts the situation as it is and refuses to become upset over it. Throughout the book he uses over and over the words "there is nothing better for a man than that he should eat and drink and take pleasure in all his toil." Although he accepts a kind of fatalism according to which there is a definite time and place for everything that happens under the sun, his book is filled with advice about how one should live in order to get the greatest enjoyment out of life. Above all else he counsels moderation. He says, "Be not righteous overmuch." But neither should one be wicked overmuch. There is always a happy medium which one should follow. One of the tragedies of life, he tells us, is for one to spend so much time and energy in preparing for old age that when it arrives he will not be able to enjoy it. One should enjoy life while he is young, for old age is characterized by weakness and infirmities which are but a prelude to the time when "the dust returns to the earth as it was, and the spirit returns to God who gave it."

Commentary

The book of Ecclesiastes is unique in many respects. One wonders how it happened that a book so skeptical in tone and so unorthodox in its contents would ever have been placed in the canon of sacred writings. Presumably there were several factors which had something to do with its inclusion among the books of the Old Testament. For one thing it made a strong appeal to many individuals because of the honesty with which the author expressed his own convictions. He knew that what he was saying was not in accord with generally accepted ideas but he had the courage to say what he believed to be true. Because the name of King Solomon had long been associated with the work of the sages it became attached to this particular piece of writing and that gave to it an added prestige. But even with these two factors in support of it, the book would probably have been excluded from the canon of scripture had it not been for an addition which appears to have been made to the last chapter. It is here that we find the words "Let us hear the conclusion of the whole matter. Fear God and keep his commandments, for this is the whole duty of man. For God shall bring every deed into judgment, whether it be good or whether it be evil."

PROVERBS
Summary

The book of Proverbs is just what the name implies. It is a collection of short sayings that have been gathered from different places and produced over long periods of time. In general they may be said to represent the wisdom that has been derived from practical experience. They contain no profound contributions to theological ideas. Instead, they constitute wholesome advice about the way one should live in order to attain a happy and satisfactory life. Late tradition attributed the entire book of Proverbs to King Solomon, but we may be sure this was not historically correct. Many of the proverbs, especially the ones which extol the virtues of monogamy, would have been most inappropriate coming from one who is reported to have had so many wives. Solomon may have been the author of some of the proverbs included in the book, but we may be quite certain that most of them originated from some other source. Within the book itself there are different collections of proverbs, some of them being attributed to men who were not Hebrews. This fact gives added emphasis to the universal character of the work of the sages. The topics which they discuss are in no sense peculiar to the Hebrew people. The wisdom that is contained in our present book of Proverbs can be said to have been drawn from a wide range of experiences, including those of both Jews and non-Jews.

The book in its present form is made up of a number of different collections. The first one, which is found in chapters 1-9, consists of a series of instructions given by a father to his son. The purpose of the Instruction is that of guiding youth "in wise dealing, righteousness, justice, and equity; that prudence may be given to the simple, knowledge and discretion to the youth." The second collection, which is entitled "The Proverbs of Solomon," is found in chapters 10-22. These proverbs are usually in couplet form and they are quite different from the ones included in the first section. It is this collection that probably constituted the original core of the book. If this be true, we may regard the first nine chapters as an appropriate introduction to the entire collection and the remaining sections as appendices added to the others. The short sections found in chapters 22-24 are most likely to be accounted for in this way, since they bear the titles "The Words of the Wise" and "These also are Words of the Wise." Chapters 25-29 begin, "These also are Proverbs which the men of Hezekiah Copied." In the last two chapters of the book we have two groups of sayings which are called "The Words of Agur, the son of Jakeh of Massa" and "The Words of King Lemuel of Massa." Since both of these men have Arabian rather than Jewish names, the inclusion of their proverbs in the final collection indicates a recognition on the part of the editors that genuine wisdom could be obtained through sources that were other than Hebrew. The book of Proverbs closes with a significant alphabetical poem written in praise of a worthy wife.

Throughout the entire book, wisdom is mentioned in terms of highest praise. The following statement is typical: "Above all things get wisdom;

whatever else you get, get understanding. Prize her and she will exalt you; embrace her and she will bring you to honor."

The wisdom to which reference is made is in one sense a human achievement, but it is also something more than that. It is of divine origin. It has its source in the deity, even though it must be received and understood by human minds. All through the book of Proverbs it is assumed that divine revelation is communicated to individuals through careful and correct thinking as well as through prophetic inspiration. This conception leads to the view that it is the wise man who lives in harmony with the divine will and it is the fool who brings disaster upon himself. The concept of wisdom is so closely related to that of the deity that in some instances it is personified and said to have been the divine agent involved in the creation of the world. It is important to note, however, that this emphasis on wisdom was not intended as an encouragement to original thinking. It was the wisdom which had been received by the men of old that should be passed on from one generation to another.

The practical character of the book of Proverbs can be seen in the instruction which is given concerning the type of conduct that should be observed in the affairs of daily living. The wise man is described as one who looks to the future and makes his plans for the present in the light of it. He does not squander his time or his money on mere pleasures of the moment. He is a hard worker who does not try to gain his livelihood by infringing on the rights of other people. He is diligent in his business, courteous to friends and neighbors, and one who governs well the affairs of his own household. He is generous in his giving, although he does not lavish gifts on those who have failed to put forth efforts to supply their own needs. He is temperate in his habits, respectful of the rights of others, and obedient of the laws of the land.

Commentary

The book of Proverbs has sometimes been regarded as a kind of textbook in the field of ethics. While it avoids any theoretical discussion concerning the basis for determining what is right or wrong, it advocates a very high standard of personal conduct. The man of wisdom will abstain from idle gossip, he will not seek the company of idle men, nor will he ever testify falsely before the judges of the land. He will avoid loose women as he would the plague. He will not waste his time in idleness, but he will use his leisure hours to reflect on the meaning of life and the paths of conduct which he should follow. He is well aware of the fact that life has its hardships, but unlike the authors of Job and Ecclesiastes, he believes that happiness and material prosperity are distributed according to merit.

It is the lazy man or the fool who comes to want, and the distress and suffering which he experiences are exactly what he deserves. On the other hand Yahweh rewards the wise and the prudent with the good things of life.

The proverbs express the conviction that loyalty to Yahweh is extremely important. In this respect they are in full agreement with the teachings of the Hebrew prophets. They differ, however, in that they define this loyalty in terms of personal conduct rather than national policy. While the authors of the book of Proverbs do place a great deal of emphasis on the selfish motive as a means of promoting good conduct, it must be remembered that this motive, though not the highest, is better than no motive at all. It is always possible that its use may bring one to the place where a higher one will be effective.

MISCELLANEOUS WRITINGS

In addition to the writings of the prophets and the sages, there are several other books which were finally included in the canon of the Old Testament. These can scarcely be classified according to any one basic characteristic. They represent different styles of writing and they have to do with a variety of subjects. These books were regarded as inspired writings but not on as high a level as the law and the prophets. Some of them were of relatively late origin and it was not until after the beginning of the Christian era that agreement was reached concerning their inclusion among the sacred writings. The books included in this group are the stories of Jonah, Ruth, and Esther, the book of Daniel, the collection of Psalms, a love poem called Song of Songs, and a book called Lamentations.

JONAH, RUTH, AND ESTHER

Summary

The book of Jonah, although often classified with the prophets, is not a prophetic book. It is a story about a prophet named Jonah. The story was written for the purpose of exposing to criticism and rebuke the narrow spirit of nationalism which he had observed among so many of the Jewish people. To accomplish this purpose he constructed a story which would illustrate the spirit he wished to counteract. Jonah in the story acted in a manner which was similar to the way the Jewish people had behaved in their attitude toward the foreign nations. Anyone reading the story could not help but see how foolish it was for Jonah to act that way. It was the author's hope that the Jewish nationalists would see themselves in the role which Jonah played.

In the story Jonah is told to go to Nineveh, the capital city of the Assyrian empire, and deliver a message which Yahweh had entrusted to him. Jonah refuses to go to Nineveh but instead he flees to Joppa, where he enters a boat that is bound for Tarshish. The ship on which he is riding encounters a storm and the men in charge, in order to save themselves, throw Jonah overboard. He is swallowed by a whale but this does not mean the end for him. He not only lives inside the whale but is carried to shore and thrown out on the land. When the call comes to him the second time to go to Nineveh, he very reluctantly obeys, but the only message which he proclaims is one of destruction which will be visited on the Ninevites because of their sins. When the people of Nineveh hear what he has to say they repent of their sins, expressing their remorse by sitting in sackcloth and ashes. This repentance on their part makes the threatened punishment unnecessary. This is a great disappointment to Jonah for it means that he has not judged them correctly. He starts to feel sorry for himself and complains to Yahweh of his bitter lot. At this point Yahweh rebukes him in no uncertain terms, explaining that the lot of one hundred and twenty thousand people is a matter of more importance than the comfort and vanity of a single individual.

The book of Ruth is a masterpiece of storytelling. Like the book of Jonah, it does have a moral lesson but this may not be the chief reason why it was written. It is a story about a Hebrew woman named Naomi who was living during the period of the judges prior to the establishment of the monarchy. After the death of her husband she went with her two sons to the land occupied by the Moabites. Here the two sons married daughters of the Moabites. Later, after both of the sons had died Naomi decides to return to the land of the Hebrews so that she might dwell among her own people. She urges the two daughters-in-law to stay with the Moabites while she goes back to her former home. One of them, named Orpah, yields to the request and bids farewell to the mother-in-law. The other one, Ruth, refuses to let the mother-in-law go back alone. Her affection and loyalty is expressed in the words "for whither thou goest, I will go; and where thou lodgest I will lodge: thy people shall be my people, and thy God my God."

As the two women journeyed back to the land of the Hebrews they came near to Bethlehem at the time of the grain harvest. Naomi's kinsman, a wealthy Hebrew named Boaz, was the owner of a large field of grain. Ruth asked that she be allowed to work with the gleaners, who gathered the grain that had been missed by the reapers. The request was granted and Boaz gave instructions to his servants to see to it that plenty of grain would be left for Ruth and her mother-in-law. Because Naomi was a relative of Boaz, she and Ruth were treated generously. In time Ruth became the wife of Boaz and their son Obed was the grandfather of King David.

The story of Esther is unique in several respects. It is not written for the purpose of setting forth any important moral or religious ideals. No mention is made of the deity nor is anything said about rewards for righteous living or punishment for evil deeds. It is a story about a Jewish maiden named Esther who was made queen in the court of the Persian king Xerxes and who was instrumental in the defeat of a plot which was intended to bring about a wholesale slaughter of the Jewish people. In the end it was the people who had plotted against the Jews who suffered defeat while at the same time the Jews achieved a remarkable victory over their enemies. The story resembles in many respects the typical historical novel, for while there may be some basis in history for the events which are related, the details of the account cannot be regarded as historical fact. The author has constructed the kind of story that was suited to the purpose which he had in mind.

The setting of the story is in the court of the Persian king. It opens with an account of a royal feast which lasted for seven days. On the last day the king asked his queen, Vashti, to display her royal beauty before the guests. She refuses and the king becomes so angry that he issues a decree that a new queen shall reign in her place. To this end he orders that beautiful maidens shall be brought to his court from various parts of his realm and from these one shall be selected as the new queen. A Jew named Mordecai has a beautiful niece named Esther whom he presents along with the others before the king, taking special care not to reveal the fact that she is a Jewess. After Esther has been made queen, her uncle, who is now employed as one of the king's gatekeepers, learns of a plot which has been made against the king's life. He reports it to Esther, who makes it known to the king, and the plotters are put to death.

In the meantime a man named Haman has been promoted to a very high place in the government and orders have been given that whenever he passes by people must bow to him. Mordecai, because of his Jewish scruples, refuses to do so and this makes Haman angry and determined to get rid of him. He persuades the king to pass a decree that on a certain day all of the Jews are to be slaughtered. Realizing the terrible plight in which his people have been placed by this decree, Mordecai pleads with Esther to go before the king and intercede in their behalf. It is a dangerous mission for her to undertake but she is willing to risk her life in order to carry it out. Haman is delighted that the king has issued this decree and in anticipation of the slaughter being carried out he constructs a gallows, on which Mordecai is to be hung. During the night when the king was unable to sleep he gave orders to his servants to read to him from the official records. They come across the account of the plot against the king's life which had been revealed by Mordecai, thus saving the life of the king. When the king finds that nothing has been done to reward the man who had saved him, he begins to wonder what would constitute an appropriate reward for one who has rendered such a great service. Seeing Haman outside, the king calls him in and asks what should be done for one "whom the king delights to honor." Haman, supposing that he is the one to be honored suggests a series of elaborate things to be done. When he has finished, the king orders that all these shall be done to honor Mordecai. In the end Haman is hanged on the very gallows which he had prepared for Mordecai, and on the day which had been originally appointed for the slaughter of the Jews the decree was reversed and the Jews were permitted and encouraged to slaughter their enemies.

Commentary

Although the prophetic period in Israel's history came to a close and it was no longer possible to make a direct declaration concerning the word of Yahweh, the ideals which had been proclaimed by the earlier prophets still persisted. It was necessary, however, to find new literary forms for their expression. One of these consisted in the short story in which the message the author had in mind could be given concrete illustration. There were many advantages to be gained from this type of writing. Because it was not necessary to report accurate historical events in every detail of the story, the author was free to construct the characters and events in a way that would illustrate precisely the lesson he wanted to teach. In the book of Jonah the author has selected a person who was reported to have lived during the times of the prophet Amos. The story which he wrote concerning this man was designed to illustrate the attitude which the Jewish people had taken toward the foreign nations. Jonah behaved so badly in the story that the average reader would become quite disgusted with him. By making it obvious that Jonah's behavior toward the Ninevites was typical of the Jewish nation as a whole, it was hoped that the effect of the story would do something to counteract the narrow nationalism of the Israelite people.

Jonah's call to go to the people of Nineveh was analogous to what the author believed Yahweh had wanted the people of Israel to do. Like Deutero-Isaiah he held that it was Israel's function to "carry true religion to the ends of the earth." But Israel had tried to run away from her responsibility. In the end she had been swallowed by Babylon, but just as Jonah had survived his experience in the whale, so Israel had returned to her own land. Still, she felt reluctant to carry out her mission to the other nations. When she did come into contact with foreign nations her only message was a warning of coming destruction. The author of the story did not believe that the foreign nations were inferior to the Hebrews or that Yahweh was prejudiced against them. If they were given the opportunity to learn of Yahweh's ways they would respond as well as the Hebrews had done. It was absurd to think that Hebrew pride was more important than the welfare of vast numbers of people.

The book of Ruth is another short story written in the interests of internationalism. The main purpose of the story was to protest against the enforcement of the law forbidding intermarriages between Hebrews and foreigners. This law was being used under the leadership of Ezra and Nehemiah to help restore loyalty on the part of those who had grown careless with reference to the observance of Hebrew rites and ceremonies. They went so far as to demand that those who had married foreigners must either get a divorce or leave the community. In many instances this involved real hardships on account of the breaking up of family relationships. In the story of Ruth an attempt was made to show that in ancient times Yahweh did not disapprove of foreign marriages. The setting of the story is placed during the period of the judges, although the story itself was of post-exilic origin. The late origin of the story is clearly indicated by the fact that one of the customs to which reference is made is said to have been one which prevailed in ancient times. Throughout the story no indication is given of any divine displeasure over foreign marriages. The two daughters of the Moabites, Ruth and Orpah, are described as persons of excellent character. They were loyal and devoted to their husbands and in every respect the equal of wives chosen from among the Hebrews. The marriage of Ruth and Boaz was blessed with children, one of whom was the grandfather of King David. Since it was from the line of David that the Messiah was to be born, it was inconceivable that Yahweh would forbid foreign marriages.

The story of Esther, unlike the other two, is illustrative of the spirit of Jewish nationalism. It is a patriotic rather than a religious story and for this reason there was some question about its inclusion with the other books in the Old Testament. Its admission to the canon of sacred scriptures is believed to be due primarily to the fact that it contains an account of the origin of the feast of Purim. The setting for the story is placed in the days of the Persian king Xerxes. The author evidently drew upon his imagination for the details of the story, since there is no evidence among the Persian records of a Jewish maiden becoming a queen in a Persian court. However, this does not matter, since historical accuracy was not the purpose of the story. It was designed to illustrate the antagonism between foreign nations and the Jews. This is shown in the stories concerning Mordecai and Haman, especially in the plot which the latter had formed in order to have the Jews massacred. Esther's decision to risk her own life in order to save her people from this plot is the noblest point of the story. Probably the author also had in mind that in the long run the Jews would be victorious over their enemies.

DANIEL

Summary

The book of Daniel is the chief example of apocalyptic writing in the Old Testament. This form of writing came into use largely in response to the disappointments which had been experienced by the Hebrews. For centuries they had looked forward to a reign of justice and righteousness on the earth. Instead of these hopes being realized, the lot of the Hebrew people was becoming more difficult with each generation, while at the same time the forces of evil were constantly becoming stronger. These circumstances led to a conviction that only a supernatural intervention by Yahweh himself would ever bring about the desired goal. Prior to this time the forces of evil would continue to grow stronger and persecutions of the righteous would become even more severe. At the appointed time a great catastrophic event would engulf the world. The wicked would be destroyed and the messianic kingdom would be established for all time to come. The purpose of the apocalyptic literature was to offer encouragement to the righteous to remain true and faithful to the principles of their religion. This would be done by giving to them the assurance that the time was not far distant when their deliverance would be at hand.

One of the chief characteristics of the apocalypses was an account of a dream or vision that had been given to someone who lived a long time before the date of writing. In this vision a series of predictions had been made concerning events that were to take place before the setting up of the messianic kingdom. All of these predictions have come to pass exactly as outlined in the vision, with the exception of the last ones before the coming of the catastrophic event. The recital of these fulfillments would inspire confidence that the remaining ones would take place in the near future. Apparently it was assumed by the apocalyptic writers that Yahweh knew the future as well as the past and he could reveal these secrets to individuals who were chosen to receive them. These predictions had to do with specific events and with definite time periods, thus indicating the exact time when particular events would occur. The occasion for the writing of an apocalypse was always a period of crisis during which the righteous people were being persecuted and threatened with death at the hands of their enemies.

It was the persecution of the Jews under Antiochus Epiphanes that led to the writing of the book of Daniel. It was during this period of crisis that the Jews were threatened with death if they refused to worship images, continued to offer prayers to Yahweh, observed their dietary laws, worshiped on the Sabbath day, or did many of the other things peculiar to their religion. Many of the Jews yielded to the demands of Antiochus and his Syrian officers in order to save their lives, but others remained faithful no matter what it might cost them to do so. It was for the encouragement of these persons whose faith was being put to so severe a test that the book of Daniel was written.

The book consists of two parts. One of these is a series of stories about Hebrews who lived at the time of the Babylonian captivity and who experienced trials similar to the ones that were being faced by the Jews under Antiochus. The other part, which is more directly apocalyptic in form, consists of a series of visions in which predictions are made concerning future events. Among the stories related in the first part of the book is one concerning four young Hebrews who refused to "eat the king's meat and to drink the king's wine," even though they had been ordered to do so and were threatened with death if they disobeyed. The young men remained faithful to the principles of their religion and as a reward for their loyalty they were not only spared any punishment for their disobedience but were given high honors and declared to be superior to the others who were in competition with them.

In another story three young Hebrews had been commanded by the king of Babylon to bow down and worship a statue that had been erected in his honor. They refused to obey this command and as a result of their decision they were thrown into a fiery furnace that had been heated to seven times its normal temperature. But Yahweh worked a miracle in their behalf and they came out of the furnace unharmed and without even the smell of smoke on their clothing. In still another story, a plot had been formed to get rid of Daniel, who though a Hebrew, held an important place in the government of King Darius. The king had been urged to sign a decree making it a capital offense for anyone, during a certain period of time, to offer prayers to any god except the one who had been designated by them. When Daniel ignored this decree and continued to pray to Yahweh with his windows open toward Jerusalem, he was thrown into a den of lions. Again Yahweh rescued his faithful servant and delivered him from the lions.

In the apocalyptic portions of the book there is recorded a series of dreams and visions which are interpreted to mean predictions concerning the rise and fall of nations from the time of the Babylonian captivity to the setting up of the messianic kingdom. In one chapter we are told about King Nebuchadnezzar's dream in which he saw a great image with a head of gold, breast and arms of silver, a belly of brass, legs of iron, and feet of iron mixed with clay. In another vision Daniel sees four beasts coming up out of the sea. One of them is a lion with eagle's wings. It is followed by a bear with three ribs in its mouth. The third beast is a leopard with four heads and four wings, and the fourth beast is described as great and terrible. It has seven heads and ten horns and among these there comes up another horn with eyes like the eyes of a man and a mouth speaking terrible things. Other visions include one of a ram and a he-goat. Prophetic periods of 2,300 days, 70 weeks, 1,235 days, and other specific periods of time are described and interpreted. Toward the end of the book we find one of the first references to a definite resurrection of the dead.

Commentary

Daniel has sometimes been classified with the prophetic books of the Old Testament, but this is a mistake owing largely to a failure to distinguish between the predominant characteristics of prophetic and apocalyptic writings. Daniel belongs to the latter group, a type of writing which in many respects stands in sharp contrast with prophetic literature. For one thing, the predictions of coming events in the apocalyptic writings are definite and specific, thus indicating the precise time when certain events will occur, whereas the predictions made in the prophetic writings are of a general nature and they are always conditioned by the decisions of people with reference to moral issues. In other words, the statements which the prophets made concerning the future were always consistent with the free choice of human beings but this was not true of the apocalypses. So far as they were concerned, what had been predicted would necessarily come to pass and there was nothing anyone could do that would alter the situation. The impression that predictions made in the distant past had been fulfilled so accurately was made possible by the fact that the apocalypses were written after these events had taken place, but they are presented as though they had been made prior to these events.

In the book of Daniel the evidence would seem to support the idea that it was written during the period of the Maccabean wars, but much of it is presented as though it had been revealed to one of the Hebrews who was involved in the Babylonian captivity. Nebuchadnezzar's dream is interpreted to mean a prediction concerning the rise and fall of four great world empires. The first one is the kingdom of Babylon, the second is that of the Medes and Persians, the third is the kingdom of Greece, and the fourth is none other than the monstrous power under whom the Jews were suffering persecution at the hands of Antiochus. The stone which is cut out of the mountain and which strikes the image on its feet, grinding it to pieces, symbolizes the destruction of this evil power and the setting up of the messianic kingdom. The same set of predictions is made again in Daniel's vision of the four beasts coming up out of the sea. In this vision a more specific characterization is given of Antiochus and the power which he represents. He is designated by the little horn which came up among the ten horns, rooting up three of them in order to make room for itself. It was this horn that had eyes like a man and a mouth speaking great things. It spoke words of blasphemy against the Most High, persecuted the saints, and endeavored to change times and laws. A further account of this same evil power is given in the vision of the ram and the he-goat. The specific time periods such as the 2,300 days, the 1,260 years, 70 weeks, etc., all have reference to the time when this evil power will be destroyed through supernatural intervention and when the new kingdom of righteousness will be set up. The reference to a resurrection from the dead indicates that this idea was beginning to find acceptance among the Hebrews.

PSALMS

Summary

The book of Psalms is said to be the most widely read and the most highly treasured of all the books in the Old Testament. It is a collection of poems, hymns, and prayers that express the religious feelings of Hebrew individuals throughout the various periods of their national history. The intrinsic beauty of the poems as well as the sentiments which they convey have contributed toward their appreciation. They are especially adapted for use in services of worship and they have been used for this purpose in Christian churches as well as in Jewish temples and synagogues. It has been said that poetry is the language of the heart and it is in this respect that the book of Psalms has a special significance for understanding the religious life of ancient Israel. The prophets and the sages give us some insight concerning what the Hebrews thought, but it is in the psalms that we have the clearest indication of what they felt. It is here that we find a revelation of the hopes, the joys, the sorrows, the loyalties, the doubts, and the aspirations of the human heart.

It is difficult to classify the psalms because of the wide variety of experiences and sentiments reflected in them. There is a further difficulty in trying to reconstruct the background or historical situation from which the different ones were produced. In the case of the prophets this can usually be done with a fair degree of accuracy but this is not true of the psalms. They represent the inner life of individuals who lived under differing circumstances and who reacted in various ways to the critical situations which developed throughout the entire course of Israel's history. They did not think alike nor did they feel the same way toward the rites and ceremonies which they had observed. It would be helpful if we could know the exact circumstances which are reflected in the different psalms, but the best we can do in this respect is to find the particular occasions for which the individual psalms would seem to be most appropriate. The book as a whole may be regarded as a kind of epitome of the entire range of the religious life of the Hebrews. It has been said that if all the rest of the Old Testament should be lost the essential faith of the Israelite people could be recovered from this single book.

The authorship of most of the psalms is anonymous, although tradition has long attributed the entire collection to King David. It is possible, but not probable, that he may have written some of them. Recent excavations and discoveries indicate quite clearly that parallels to certain of the psalms were in existence as early as the period of the monarchy and the fact that David has been referred to as the "sweet singer of Israel" lends some support to the tradition. However, most of the psalms reflect ideas and conditions which came into existence long after the times of King David. One psalm in particular has to do with an event which occurred during the life of Isaiah. Others describe experiences pertaining to the Babylonian captivity, and still others appear to have had their origin during the period of the Maccabean wars. It seems probable that the earliest collection of psalms was entitled "Psalms of David" and to this group several others were added at various times. These include what was known as the "Korah Psalter," the "Asaph Psalter," the "Hallelujah Psalter," the "Pilgrim Psalter," and others. The book in its present form is divided into five sections. The first one includes chapters 1-41, the second, chapters 42-72, the third, chapters 73-89, the fourth, chapters 90-106, and the fifth, chapters 107-150.

The psalms were used in connection with the worship services that were conducted in the Temple at Jerusalem. Some of them were sung by the pilgrims on their journeys to the Central Sanctuary, for all of the faithful were required to attend services at this place at least once a year if it was at all possible for them to do so. Some of the hymns would be sung when they first came in sight of the city of Jerusalem and others as they stood before the entrance into the Temple. Some of the hymns used were antiphonal numbers and their use constituted an essential part of the worship service. Hymns and prayers of adoration were used on appropriate occasions, such as the beginning of the new year, particular feast days, the enthronement of Yahweh, and celebrations of important events in Hebrew history. There were songs of praise to Yahweh for the mighty works which he had performed in their behalf. There were songs of thanksgiving for the way in which the Hebrews had been delivered from the hands of their enemies. Other songs were written in praise of the law.

Many different themes are treated in the book of Psalms. Psalm 46 praises Yahweh for coming to the defense of his people at the time when the Assyrian armies had invaded Judah, capturing forty-six of the fenced cities. The sudden withdrawal of the army, leaving the city of Jerusalem standing, was indeed an occasion for great rejoicing. Yahweh's love for the poor and the oppressed is the theme of Psalm 146. Sorrow and discouragement because of the fate which had befallen the nation when the people were taken into captivity by a foreign power is expressed in the prayers which are recorded in chapters 42 and 43. The same attitude can be found in Psalm 22, where the author cries out from the depths of his soul: "My God, my God, why hast thou forsaken me?" In the midst of the Babylonian captivity we find the setting for Psalm 137, which reports "We hung our harps on the willows and wept when we remembered Zion." Psalm 119, the longest one in the entire book, is an alphabetical poem written in praise of the law.

It would be difficult to summarize the teachings of the Psalms, since their main purpose was not instruction but expressions of the heart made in the spirit of worship. Nevertheless, there are certain ideas set forth in the Psalms which are essential to the purpose for which they were written. One of these is the reality and significance of Yahweh in relation to the experiences of individuals and the nation as a whole. It is true that the conception of Yahweh is not always the same in the different psalms, but this is due to the fact that each author must find for himself the conception which seems most adequate to him. Sometimes Yahweh is portrayed as a god of loving kindness and mercy, but at other times he is a god of wrath who brings destruction on those who disobey his commands. Always Yahweh is presented as an everlasting God, one who is omnipotent, omniscient, and one whose power and goodness endure throughout all generations.

Commentary

The collection of the Psalms and their preservation in the canon of sacred scriptures gives to the modern reader an insight into the religious life of the Hebrews that cannot be obtained from any of the other writings. It is true that Jeremiah and some of the other prophets emphasized the inwardness of religion, but they did it primarily to counteract the formalism that had become conspicuous in the Temple services and other practices which they observed. It is in the Psalms that the longings, the hopes, the sorrows, and the disappointments of individual worshipers find their clearest expression. It is here that we find what the various authors felt even in those situations which they were not able to understand. Although some of the psalms are probably as old as the times of King David, it was not until a relatively late period that the entire collection was gathered and organized in the form in which they have been preserved to the present time.

Like other portions of Old Testament literature, the original psalms were edited and supplemented from time to time. Frequently we find evidence of a tendency to add something to the psalm as it first appeared in order to give to it an interpretation that would be more in accord with generally accepted ideas. An interesting example of this kind can be seen in Psalm 51. The first seventeen verses of this psalm were written in the spirit of the great prophets, who insisted that the true worship of Yahweh consisted not in sacrifices made on an altar nor in the observance of ritualistic requirements but in the inner attitudes of the human heart. The next two verses of the psalm present a very different idea, for an editor who was evidently under the influence of the post-exilic emphasis on the importance of ritual and ceremony added a statement which was intended to show that the attitude of the human heart was but a prelude to the sacrificing of bulls on the altar. It is not uncommon, even at the present time, to find hymn books which continue to use ancient conceptions, even though these have long been replaced with ideas that are more nearly in harmony with the spirit of the times. This is especially true of the book of Psalms.

LAMENTATIONS AND THE SONG OF SONGS
Summary

The fall of the city of Jerusalem and the fate of the captives who were led into exile forms the subject matter of the book of Lamentations. There are five poems included in the book and they may have been written by as many different individuals. All of the poems have to do with the destruction of the city and the events closely related to that event. It was a terrifying experience and one that put to a severe test the faith of those who had put their trust in Yahweh. The poems portray some of the horrors that had been experienced. The city had been placed under siege, famine had driven the people to despair, and when king Zedekiah and a band of his soldiers tried to escape during the night, they were overtaken by the Babylonians and brought before Nebuchadnezzar for punishment. Zedekiah was forced to witness the execution of his own sons. He was then blinded and taken to a Babylonian dungeon for the rest of his life. The suffering caused by the famine and the bitter anxiety brought on by the terrible fate of Judah's last king were clearly in the mind of the poet who wrote one of the chapters included in the book. The poem closes with a prediction that Edom, who in the hour of Judah's agony had given her support to the Babylonians, would meet her doom in the very near future.

In another poem an attempt is made to understand the reason for this terrible tragedy which had befallen the Hebrew people. The author bemoans the ruin that Yahweh has wrought in his anger. He then addresses the people of Zion, blaming the prophets for the miserable plight that has evoked only scorn from the enemies of Israel and calling upon the people to weep and to cry to Yahweh for mercy. A third poem which is an acrostic in structure and style is placed in the center of the book and the others are arranged with reference to it. The last chapter of the book contains a prayer in which someone who has survived the catastrophe implores Yahweh for mercy and help.

The Song of Songs is not a religious book. It is a collection of secular love poems and wedding songs. They portray the scenes of a typical Oriental wedding feast. The bridegroom is a king, the bride is a queen and the feast lasts for a period of seven days. The songs celebrate the physical beauty of the royal pair, especially the bride. There is nothing in any of these songs concerning the sanctity of marriage or any of the moral and spiritual aspects associated with it. They are about human love with all of its passion and deep emotion. One of the songs has to do with the springtime of love. It is full of erotic suggestiveness which is usually offensive to the Occidental mind. It should be remembered, however, that physical love was regarded as neither base nor obscene by the Oriental. It was an important factor in human life and a proper theme to be celebrated in poetry. It is extremely unlikely that these poems would ever have been included in the Old Testament had it not been for the allegorical interpretation which was placed on them.

Commentary

The authorship of the book of Lamentations is unknown. The earliest collection of the poems included in the book was called "Lamentations" without assigning any name to them. Later, they were called "The Lamentations of Jeremiah," and this is the title that has been given to them in various editions of the Old Testament. The Greek translation states in the preface to the book: "And it came to pass, after Israel was led into captivity and Jerusalem laid waste, that Jeremiah sat weeping, and lamented with this lamentation over Jerusalem." There is nothing in the book of Jeremiah that would indicate he was the author of these poems and we may be quite sure they were produced by other persons. Since Jeremiah was regarded by later generations as an inspired author, attributing these poems to him would give to them an added prestige and this was probably the reason why it was done.

The Song of Songs was attributed to King Solomon, probably because his name is mentioned several times in the poems. Since the songs describe the wedding feast of a king and his bride, it was assumed that the chief participants in the wedding were King Solomon and a Shulamite maiden. Interpreted literally these songs would scarcely have been included in the books of the Old Testament. But it was possible to interpret them allegorically and find their meaning in the relationship between Yahweh and his people. As the Hebrew people understood the songs, it was Yahweh who was the bridegroom and Israel was the bride. In later generations Christians interpreted the same songs as representing the union between Christ and his church. We have no reason for thinking that King Solomon or any single poet was the author of these songs. They are a group of folk songs, some of which may have been in existence for a long time before they were edited and arranged in their present form, which was probably sometime during the third century B.C.

THE APOCRYPHA AND THE PSEUDEPIGRAPHA

When the author of Ecclesiastes wrote, "Of making many books there is no end, and much study is a weariness of the flesh," he apparently thought that everything worth knowing had already been written and there was nothing to be gained by writing more books. But writing did not cease with the completion of his manuscript. So far as the Hebrew people were concerned, each succeeding generation continued to write books and many of these were regarded as worthy of inclusion along with the other writings that were destined to become a part of the Old Testament. Eventually it became necessary to decide which writings were to be accepted as the authoritative word of Yahweh and which ones should be excluded from the list of inspired or sacred scriptures. The decision was not reached all at once. Some of the writings were accepted without question, while others were regarded as somewhat doubtful, and there were still others that were not accepted at all. It required several centuries before there was any general agreement among the Jewish rabbis concerning all of the books which are now included in the Old Testament. Apparently the majority of the Jewish people accepted the idea of degrees of inspiration. For example, the so-called books of Moses, known as the Torah, or the books of the Law, were regarded as the most highly inspired and therefore the most authoritative of all the writings. Next to the Law came the group of prophetic books which included the historical writings as well as the ones named for the prophets. These were considered to be inspired and authoritative but on a somewhat lower level than the books of the Law. A third group, known as the Hagiographa, or miscellaneous writings, while still inspired and authoritative, were believed to be on a level that was somewhat lower than that of the prophets. In addition to these books, there were two more groups of writings recognized as valuable and appropriate for use even in religious service but not used as authoritative sources for the establishment of doctrine. These were known as the Apocrypha and the Pseudepigrapha, both of which are relevant to the study of the Old Testament.

The Apocrypha is the name given to a group of writings found in some versions of the Old Testament but not in others. At the present time they are usually included in the Catholic Bibles but not in the Protestant ones. They were, however, included in Protestant versions until the second quarter of the nineteenth century. When in the year 382 A.D., Jerome was commissioned by the Pope to make a new translation of the Scriptures, he went to Palestine rather than to Alexandria in Egypt to obtain copies of the original. In doing this he discovered that fourteen of the books included in the Alexandrian, or Greek, versions of the Old Testament were missing in the Palestinian version. The question then arose concerning the status of these books. The name Apocrypha, which means "hidden things," was given to them because it was believed the men who wrote them were not addressing their contemporaries but were writing for the benefit of future generations. Hence, the meaning of the books would be hidden until their interpretation would be disclosed at some future date by persons qualified to make it.

The books in the Apocrypha include histories, short stories, wisdom literature, and additions to canonical books. Among the historical writings are I and II Maccabees, and I and II Esdras. The two books of Maccabees contain accounts of the Maccabean wars written from different points of view. I Maccabees tells the story from what came to be known as the position of the Sadducees and II Maccabees reflects the position of the Pharisee party. The two books of Esdras are apocalyptic in character but they portray certain aspects of Jewish history. These are presented as though they were fulfillments of predictions made in the distant past. The Wisdom Literature includes Ecclesiasticus, or what has sometimes been called the Wisdom of Jesus ben Sirach. It resembles the book of Proverbs in many respects, although it covers many more topics. It concludes with a famous discourse introduced by the words "Come now and let us praise famous men." The author includes himself in the list of Israel's most famous men. Another book called The Wisdom of Solomon appears to have been written as a reply to the argument given in the book of Ecclesiastes. In it the author affirms his belief in Yahweh, whose activities he finds illustrated throughout the course of Hebrew history. It is also interesting to note that he believes in a life after death.

The short stories of the Apocrypha are called Tobit and Judith. Tobit, called Tobias in some versions, tells about Jews who have been faithful to the ritualistic requirements of their religion and have been abundantly rewarded for their good works. Judith, which in many ways is similar to the book of Esther, tells about a Jewish woman living in the city of Jerusalem at a time when the city is besieged by the Assyrians and her people are in a desperate situation. She is not only a faithful Jewess but a courageous person who invades the camp of the enemy and succeeds in a plot which enables the Jews to achieve a remarkable victory. Several additions to the book of Daniel are included in the Apocrypha. One of these, called the Prayer of Azariah, is said to be a record of the prayer which was offered by one of the Hebrews who was thrown into the fiery furnace by King Nebuchadnezzar. Another one called the Song of the Three Children claims to be the song of praise which was sung by these same Hebrews as an expression of gratitude for the marvelous way in which they were delivered. The History of Susanna tells of a woman who has been accused unjustly of the sin of adultery. The wickedness of her accusers as well as the innocence of the woman is established by the prophet Daniel. The story of Bel and the Dragon tells how Daniel was delivered from the hands of his enemies, who were trying to have him put to death. An addition to the book of Esther reports a dream given to Mordecai in which forthcoming events were revealed to him. The Book of Baruch is an addition to the book of Jeremiah. In some versions it contains a section called an Epistle of Jeremiah. The Prayer of Manasseh supplements a story recorded in the book of Chronicles, telling how this king who had done so many wicked things during his life repented of his sins before he died.

The term *Pseudepigrapha* is used to designate a group of writings each one of which is attributed to someone other than the real author. Many writings of this kind appeared during the centuries immediately preceding and immediately following the beginning of the Christian era. Most of these were apocalyptic in character, which means that they were regarded as revelations of things to come which had been given to worthy individuals who lived in the distant past. In several instances they reflect the legalistic attitude which was especially strong among the majority of the Jews during those periods when they were subject to the domination of the Roman government. This type of literature was in use during New Testament times and there are references to books in both the Apocrypha and the the Pseudepigrapha in the books of the New Testament.

The most important of the apocalyptic writings in this collection is the Book of Enoch, a relatively late book but one which was attributed to Enoch who was the seventh from Adam. Visions are said to have been given to him in which he received revelations concerning all sorts of mysteries pertaining to both heaven and earth. One section of the book contains the Apocalypse of Weeks, which tells of a vision in which there was revealed to Enoch the whole course of history from creation to the setting up of the messianic kingdom. The Testament of the Twelve Patriarchs, which purports to have come from the twelve sons of Jacob, contains a series of predictions concerning the future of each of the twelve tribes of Israel. The Sibylline Oracles is a collection of so-called revelations made to ancient prophetesses but which have been edited and rewritten in the light of contemporary events.

The Assumption of Moses is another apocalypse. It is written as though it were an address delivered by Moses to his successor. In the vision which was given to Moses shortly before his death the whole course of Hebrew history was revealed in advance. The final triumph of the people of Israel will be brought about through supernatural intervention. In the Secrets of Enoch an account is given of a dream-vision in which Enoch is transported through a series of heavens into the presence of the deity. It is here that many of the mysteries concerning the created universe are explained to him and a statement is made concerning the length of time which will elapse before the setting up of the messianic kingdom. Further examples of apocalyptic writing are II and III Baruch and IV Ezra. They are concerned primarily with such questions as the origin of evil and the way in which it will finally be banished from the universe.

Not all of the writings in the Pseudepigrapha are of an apocalyptic nature. The Psalms of Solomon is a collection of eighteen psalms which extol the Pharisaic conception of righteousness. The standard which is set forth is complete obedience to the perfect law of God. The Fourth Book of Maccabees has to do with the field of ethics. It is a discourse on the power of reason to control the passions and illustrations are drawn from the experiences of such men as Jacob, Joseph, Moses, and David. The Story of Ahikar belongs to the folktales of the ancient Hebrews. The hero of the story was an official in the court of an Assyrian king. An evil plot had been formed against him by men who wished to bring about his death. The plot fails and Ahikar is able to take full revenge on his enemies. The Book of Jubilees is written in praise of the law which had been revealed to Moses. The law is declared to be everlasting and the importance of obedience to its demands is illustrated throughout the entire course of history. A somewhat different attitude toward the law is presented in the Book of Zodak which was written in support of a reform movement that was designed to counteract the formalism and irregularities of the priesthood. Among the sacred legends one finds the Letter of Aristeas, which describes the circumstances which led to the making of the Septuagint version of the Hebrew writings. The Books of Adam and Eve record popular beliefs concerning the events which followed immediately after Adam and Eve had been driven out of the Garden of Eden. Finally, the Martyrdom of Isaiah describes the way in which the prophet Isaiah met his death at the hands of the wicked king Manasseh.

IMPORTANT OLD TESTAMENT DATES

The Exodus   1250 B.C. (approximate)
Establishment of the Monarchy   1000 B.C. (approximate)
Division of the Monarchy   922 B.C.
The Northern Kingdom (Israel)   922 B.C. – 721 B.C.
The Assyrian Conquest of Israel   721 B.C.
The Southern Kingdom (Judah)   922 B.C. – 586 B.C.
First Babylonian Conquest   597 B.C.
Second Babylonian Conquest   586 B.C.
Return from the Babylonian Exile   520 B.C.
Discovery of the Law Book in the Temple   621 B.C.
The Maccabean Revolt   168 B.C. – 165 B.C.

A SELECTED BIBLIOGRAPHY

Anderson, B. W. *Understanding the Old Testament.* Englewood Clit ., N.J.: Prentice-Hall, 1957.

Bewer, Julius A. *The Literature of the Old Testament,* 3rd ed. New York: Columbia University Press, 1962.

Bright, John. *A History of Israel.* Philadelphia: Westminster Press, 1959.

Flanders, Crapps, and Smith. *People of the Covenant: An Introduction to the Old Testament.* New York: Ronald Press, 1963.

Gottwald, N. R. *A Light to the Nations.* New York: Harpers, 1959.

Harrelson, Walter. *Interpreting the Old Testament.* New York: Holt, Rinehart & Winston, 1964.

Mould, E. W. K. *Essentials of Bible History.* New York: Ronald Press, 1951.

Oesterley and Robinson. *A History of Israel.* New York: Oxford University Press, 1931.

Patterson, Charles H. *The Philosophy of the Old Testament.* New York: Ronald Press, 1953.

Pfeiffer, Robert H. *Introduction to the Books of the Old Testament.* New York: Harpers, 1957.

Robinson, H. Wheeler. *The Old Testament: Its Making and Meaning.* London: University of London Press, 1956.

Sandmel, Samuel. *The Hebrew Scriptures.* New York: Alfred A. Knopf, 1963.